STORIES OF
Dogs
AND THE
LIVES THEY TOUCH

Stories of Dogs

and the Lives They Touch

Edited by Peggy Schaefer

Ideals Publications
Nashville, Tennessee

ISBN 0-8249-4627-8

Published by Ideals Publications, a division of Guideposts
535 Metroplex Drive, Suite 250, Nashville, Tennessee 37211
www.idealsbooks.com

Printed and bound in the U.S.A. by RR Donnelley

Library of Congress CIP data on file

Publisher, Patricia A. Pingry
Associate Publisher, Peggy Schaefer
Series Designer, Marisa Calvin
Copy Editor, Melinda Rathjen

Cover photo copyright © Index Stock Imagery, Inc./Steve Puetzer.

10 9 8 7 6 5 4 3 2

ACKNOWLEDGMENTS

ATKINSON, BROOKS. "Cleo for Short." Originally appeared in the *Atlantic Monthly*. Reprinted
in *Old Dogs Remembered*. COUGHLIN, RUTH POLLACK. "Not a Bone to Pick." Originally
appeared in the *Detroit News*. Reprinted in *Old Dogs Remembered*, edited by Bud Johns.
Carroll & Graf Publishers, Inc., 1993. BASS, RICK. "Homer and Ann" from chapter two of
Colter: The True Story of the Best Dog I Ever Had. Copyright © 2000 by Rick Bass.
Reprinted by permission of Houghton Mifflin Company. HERRIOT, JAMES. "A First-Rate Dog" from
James Herriot's Dog Stories. Copyright © 1986 by James Herriot. Reprinted by permission of
St. Martin's Press, LLC and by Harold Ober Associates, Inc. for Canada. KATZ, JOHN.
"Poultrygeist" and "Welcome to Newark Airport" from *A Dog Year*. Copyright © 2002 by
John Katz. Used by permission of Villard Books, a division of Random House, Inc.
KAUFMAN, MARGO. "Clara, the Hero?" and "A Glimmer of Intelligence" from *Clara: The
Early Years*. Copyright © 1998 by Margo Kaufman. Used by permission of Villard Books, a
division of Random House, Inc. ROSE, ELISABETH. "Compact Gods" from *For the Love of a
Dog*. Copyright © 2001 by Elisabeth Rose. Used by permission of Harmony Books, a divi-
sion of Random House, Inc. Spinifex Press, for permission to reprint "Gypsy" by Claire
Warren, "Lyn and Ralphie" by Lyn Zboril, and "The Dogs of My Life" by Jan Fook.
Copyrights © 2001 by the authors. From *A Girl's Best Friend: The Meaning of Dogs in Women's
Lives*. Spinifex Press, Victoria, Australia, 2001.

Essays by the following authors originally appeared in *Angels On Earth*, published by
Guideposts, NY: Carter Allen, Carolyn Anne Anderson, Petina Barrett, Linda D. Baxter,
Deby Duzan, Philip Gonzalez, Betsy MacDonald, Elizabeth Polk, and Lois Spoon. Essays
by the following authors originally appeared in *Guideposts* magazine: Sharon Azar, Reldon
Bray, Grace Chamberlain, Kathleen Fornataro, Eunice Merritt, Roberta L. Messner, Stuart
Reininger, John Sherrill, Shari Smyth, Nancy Long Tafoya, and Suzanne Vaden.

All possible care has been taken to fully acknowledge the ownership and use of the selec-
tions in this book. If any mistakes or omissions have occurred, they will be corrected in
subsequent editions, provided notification is sent to the publisher.

CONTENTS

The Right Dog

at the Right Time

A First-Rate Dog

James Herriot

It was a Saturday lunchtime when Rosie came in and said excitedly, "There's an advertisement in the Darlington and Stockton Times about some Border puppies. It's a Mrs. Mason in Bedale."

The announcement burst on me like a bombshell and I was all for immediate action, but my wife's response surprised me.

"It says here," she said, studying the newspaper, "that these pups are eight weeks old, so they'd be born around Christmas. Remember you said that after waiting all this time we'd be better with a spring puppy."

"Yes, that's right," I replied. "But Helen, these are Borders! We might not get another chance for ages!"

She shrugged. "Oh, I'm sure we'll find one at the right time if only we're patient."

"But . . . but . . ." I found I was talking to Helen's back. She was bending over a pan of potatoes.

"Lunch will be ready in ten minutes," she said. "You and Rosie can take Polly for a little walk."

As we strolled along the lane outside our house, Rosie turned to me. "What a funny thing. I can't understand it. Mum is as keen as you to get another dog and yet here is a

7

litter of Borders—the very thing you've been waiting for. They're so scarce. It seems such a pity to miss them."

"I don't think we will miss them," I murmured.

"What do you mean? You heard what she said."

I smiled indulgently. "You've often heard your mother say that she knows me inside out. She can tell in advance every single thing that I'm going to do?"

"Yes but . . ."

"Well, what she forgets is that I know her inside out too. I'll lay a small bet that when we get back to the house, she'll have changed her mind."

Rosie raised her eyebrows. "I very much doubt it. She seemed very definite to me."

On our return I opened the front door and saw Helen speaking into the telephone.

She turned to me and spoke agitatedly. "I've got Mrs. Mason on the line now. There's only one pup left out of the litter and there are people coming from as far as eighty miles away to see it. We'll have to hurry. What a long time you've been out there!"

We bolted our lunch and Helen, Rosie, granddaughter Emma and I drove out to Bedale. Mrs. Mason led us into the kitchen and pointed to a tiny brindle creature twisting and writhing under the table.

"That's him," she said.

I reached down and lifted the puppy as he curled his little body round, apparently trying to touch his tail with his nose. But that tail wagged furiously and the pink tongue was busy at my hand. I knew he was ours before my quick examination for hernia and overshot jaw.

The deal was quickly struck and we went outside to inspect the puppy's relations. His mother and grandmother were out there. They lived in little barrels which served as kennels and both of them darted out and stood up at our legs, tails lashing, mouths panting in delight. I felt vastly reassured. With happy, healthy ancestors like those I knew we had every chance of a first-rate dog.

As we drove home with the puppy in Emma's arms, the warm thought came to me. The wheel had indeed turned. After nearly fifty years I had my Border terrier.

The choice of a name exercised our minds for many days with arguments, suggestions and counter-suggestions. We finally decided on "Bodie." Helen and I were great fans of the TV series, *The Professionals*, and our particular hero was Lewis Collins who took the part of Bodie. We have met Lewis a few times and were at first a little hesitant about telling him that we had named our dog after him, but he doesn't mind, knowing us and understanding the honoured place a dog occupies in our household.

Helen and I settled down happily with Bodie. We had been lost without a dog in the house, and it was a lovely relief to have filled that awful gap. It was extraordinary that the gap was filled by a grizzled, hairy-faced little creature about nine inches long, but Bodie effortlessly performed the miracle. Helen had a dog to feed again and to see to his in-house care and bedding; and I had a companion in my car and on my bedtime walk, even though he was almost invisible on the end of his lead.

His first meeting with Polly was a tremendous event. I mentioned the instant friendship between [our dogs] Hector and Dan. It was different with Bodie. He fell in love.

This is no exaggeration. Polly became and is to this day the most important living creature in his world. Since she lived next door he was able to watch her house from our sitting-room window, and a wild yapping was always the sign that the adored one had appeared in her garden. Fortunately for his peace of mind, he had a walk with her every day and at the weekends several times a day and, as he grew up, it was clear that this routine was the most significant thing in his life.

It was when he was about a year old that I was walking down a lane with the two of them trotting ahead. Memories stirred in me as I watched them—the noble Labrador and the scruffy little terrier side by side. Suddenly Polly picked up a stick, Bodie seized one end of it, and in a flash a hectic tug-of-war was raging. The little Border grumbled and growled in fierce concentration and as Polly glanced at me with amusement in her eyes, I had the uncanny impression that I had gotten Hector and Dan back again.

As Bodie approached the adult stage, I was able to assess his various qualities. My *Dog Encyclopaedia*, describing the Border, uses words like "tough," "honest," "down to earth." It does not say that it is pretty; in fact, it states that it has "not quite the elegance of the more fashionable members of the terrier group." I would have to admit all that. Bodie's shaggy, whiskered little face is almost comic, but it has certainly grown on me. When I look at it now, I can find great depths of character and expression.

The book also describes the breed as "intensely loyal and gentle with children." Again, right on both counts, but Bodie obviously regards himself as a tough guy and, as such, seems a little embarrassed about showing his affection. If I am sitting on a sofa, he will flop down almost apologetically by my side as though doing so by accident, but lying very close all the same, and he has a particular habit of creeping unobtrusively between my feet at mealtimes or when I am writing. He is down there at this moment, and since this is a swivel chair, I have to be careful about sudden turns.

One unfortunate result of his infatuation with Polly is that he has become insanely jealous. His possessiveness is such that he will hurl himself unhesitatingly at any male dog, however large, who might be a possible suitor, and this invariably leads to an embarrassing fracas followed by profuse apologies to the irate owner.

Such behavior is very unwise in one so small because he usually comes off second best. Yet he never surrenders. Only last week I removed the stitches from his shoulder after an encounter with an enormous crossbred Alsatian. By the time I dived in after Bodie's attack, this dog was waving him round in the air by one leg, but the Border, his mouth full of hair, was still looking for more trouble.

He may be foolish, but he is also very brave. My encyclopaedia points out that these little terriers have been for centuries in the Border country between Scotland and England to hunt and destroy foxes, and maybe that accounts for his total lack of fear. But, be that as it may, I have to scan the horizon carefully every time I am out with him and Polly.

However, he is by no means entirely aggressive. With lady dogs he is all charm, swaggering round them, tail high, smirking through his whiskers. And if they will consent to play with him, he behaves with the utmost gallantry as they roll him over in happy rough and tumbles. They can knock him down and jump on him at will, but he submits cheerfully, a silly half-smile on his face.

The strange twisting of his body which I observed when I first saw him has remained with him. Whenever he is pleased to see anybody, he sidles up to them almost crabwise, his tail almost touching his nose. I have never seen this characteristic in any other dog.

Since Dan was his immediate predecessor, the difference in obedience was acutely evident. The big Labrador, like most of his breed, was born with the desire to obey. He watched me anxiously all the time, longing to do my bidding, and even little things like getting out of the car or moving from one room to another had to wait for my gesture. Not so with Bodie. After prolonged effort, I have managed to get him to respond to such simple commands as "stay" or "here" and even then he does so in his own good time, but if he is really engrossed in something which interests him, he pays very little attention to me. After hearing me bawl at him about ten times he may look up at me with an expression of mild enquiry, and I find this disconcerting because people expect vets to have well-trained dogs. Recently, a little five-year-old boy, a near neighbour, informed me solemnly, "You're always shouting 'Bodie! Bodie! Bodie!'" so I fear it is part of the local pattern to hear my despairing cries echoing round our village.

And yet . . . and yet . . . the little fellow has a charisma all of his own, a scruffy appeal which seems to get under the skin of all Border owners. There aren't all that many of the breed around, and I find myself staring with the keenest interest whenever I see one in the street. I know I am not alone in this, because other owners seem to be similarly fascinated with Bodie. There is certainly a bond between us all.

Last summer I was walking Bodie outside a motel halfway between here and Glasgow when a man pushed his head out of his car window as he drew out of the park.

"That's a nice little Border!" he cried.

I swelled with unimaginable pride. "Yes, have you got one?" I called back.

"We have indeed!" He waved and was gone, but the feeling of comradeship remained.

There was another warming encounter during our spring holiday this year. I had just parked my car in the vehicle deck of the ferry which plies between Oban and the Isle of Barra in the Outer Hebrides when I noticed a silver-haired American gentleman gazing at Bodie who was stretched out in his favourite position on the back shelf.

He was another devotee and told me about his own Border. It seems they are even scarcer on the other side of the

Atlantic, and he said he knew of only three kennels of the breed in that vast country. Before he left he took another long look into my car.

"Magnificent little dogs," he murmured reverently.

He was voicing my own feelings, but when I think of Bodie I am not concerned with the merits of his breed. The thing which warms and fills me with gratitude is that he has completely taken the place of the loved animals which have gone before him. It is a reaffirmation of the truth which must console all dog owners; that the void can be filled while the good memories remain.

That is how it is with our family and Bodie. He is just as dear to us as all the others.

No Such Animal

Carter Allen

My girlfriend, Dawn, and I stayed out late into the night not long after New Year's Day. It was snowing heavily when we got into my car, and we decided to go only as far as my mother's house, about ten miles away. I drove slowly, the headlights of my compact car boring white tunnels in the swirling flakes.

Around 1:30 A.M., about a half hour after setting out, we turned onto Mom's road in a rural area near the northern Minnesota town of Walker. There were only a couple of dwellings on the two-mile stretch leading to her house, and Mom knew all the comings and goings in this quiet area.

By then the storm had become a raging blizzard. The windshield wipers groaned, protesting the mounting accumulation. Ghostly drifts shrouded the road and I tried to keep the wheel steady. I shifted into low gear and Dawn gasped. "Don't worry," I assured her. "We'll make it."

No sooner had I spoken than we hit a hidden dip. The car lurched sideways and I struggled to regain control as we shot into a ditch. "Hold on," I said. The wheels spun futilely when I pressed the accelerator. We were stuck.

"What now?" Dawn whispered.

"We'll have to shovel our way out as best we can," I said.

I reached onto the floor of the backseat. All I had was a snow brush. Dawn and I got out. Squinting against the stinging crystals, she wielded the brush and I scooped the white powder with my hands, trying desperately to free up space around the tires. But as fast as we dug, the driving snow relentlessly filled in the gaps.

We looked at each other in desperation. The wind-chill factor must have been way below zero, with the gale shrieking off the flat fields bordering the road. Our tennis shoes, jeans, sweaters, and jackets were no match for the cold. We climbed back into the car and started the engine to warm up. But in about fifteen minutes it died.

"Snow blocking the exhaust," I sighed. We sat quietly for a moment, the howling wind stealing through every possible crack. Thick frost built up on the windows.

Think, I told myself. Mom's house was still a good two miles away, too far to walk in this terrible storm.

"Remember that house about a half-mile back?" I asked Dawn. She nodded. "Maybe we can get help there."

"I can't think of any other way out," she said. "Let's go. It's worth a try."

Again we ventured into the blizzard, which had now become a whiteout, and plodded through knee-deep drifts toward the house. After some ten yards, I looked back. I couldn't see Dawn. I couldn't see more than five feet.

"Dawn!" I called. "Can you hear me?" Retracing my path, I found her. She looked dazed.

"Thought I was right behind you," she said. She wasn't going to make it. I led her back to the car, settled her in, and took off running as fast as I could to the house.

Finally I stomped onto the dark stoop and pounded on the door. After a while a porch light blinked on and a man pulled open the inner door. I saw him pull the screen door shut.

"I'm sorry to wake you," I said, "but my car is stuck in a ditch, and my girlfriend and I are stranded."

"Can't help you," the man said, his face set, and he started to push the door closed. I could see that he was old and frightened, but I tried again. "Please, I just need to use your phone."

"Don't have one," he said. "And my car doesn't work. Like I said, I can't help you." He shut the door. The light went off.

What are we going to do? Tears froze on my face as I headed back to the car. My shoulders and back tense from bracing against the driving snow, I trudged on, feeling weaker with every step. Stumbling along, I was dimly aware of something following me. But I was so exhausted, so agonizingly cold, it was all I could do to put one foot in front of the other. I didn't have the strength even to turn around and investigate. *Too much effort,* I thought sluggishly. "God," I said, "only you can help us now." Then, my head swimming in blackness, I pitched forward into a drift.

When I came to, a prickly, hairy form covered me like a blanket. *What . . . ?* Some sort of a huge black dog had lain on top of me. "Good boy," I whispered, rubbing my hands in the stiff fur under his neck. Is he wild? I wondered. No pet would be out in this weather. I looked into his eyes. He seemed somehow to want to help me, almost as if he knew why we had crossed paths.

17

I pressed my face into his thick fur and breathed the air warmed by his body. The dog stood up.

What a magnificent animal, I thought. I had never seen a similar breed. Feeling new strength, I rose and headed for the car. I half expected the dog to continue on with me, but looking back, I saw nothing; my dark rescuer had disappeared into the storm.

I found Dawn shivering. "I didn't have any luck at the house," I told her. "But on the way back, something incredible happened."

We huddled close in the back seat, and I began to describe my encounter with the mysterious black dog. "What was he like?" Dawn asked. "Was he beautiful?" I stretched out the details, making the story last. Just the telling of it warmed me, and I could feel Dawn relax in my arms.

When morning light brightened our snow-covered windows, we heard the roar of a snowplow. Then someone rapped on the glass. The Good Samaritan driver took us to my mother's house. "You were out all night in that awful storm?" Mom said. "God must have been watching over you."

I told her about the black dog who saved my life, and she looked doubtful. "I know my road," she said. "There's no such dog around here."

Then her eyes widened. "But, you know, twice I've seen a black wolf wandering around that very spot—" She stopped. She knew it as well as I did. That dog, or wolf, or whatever it was, wasn't wandering. It had been sent.

Homer and Ann

Rick Bass

A ll of my dogs have been wonderful accidents that have happened to me, and now I am drowning in dogs and it is wonderful. I go to sleep amid the sounds of dogs stirring, settling in for the night downstairs, and wake up in the early morning to their whimpers and yawns and stretches. Of the first two dogs I ever owned as an adult, one, Homer, is still with me after fifteen years. Homer and Ann were black-and-tan Mississippi hounds of some unpatented beagle and walker hound and black-and-tan mix. When I found them, they were mangy and worm-ridden, and I only meant to take them to the animal shelter.

I was driving down a back road in Mississippi at dusk when I saw two tiny pups, one slender, one heavy, sitting by the roadside next to a third pup lying dead in the road. The slender pup, wild as the wind, galloped up a narrow game trail, arched with thorns and brambles of blackberry bushes, leapt up onto the splintered porch of an old abandoned house, and darted through an open door, disappearing into the dark maw of ruin.

I followed cautiously. I searched each room, half-fearing that humans, under the most dire of straits, might still be camping in that rubble, but each room was empty. When I came to the back porch, I saw that it opened into the exuberant jungle of Mississippi in June. (The pups appeared to have just been weaned, seven weeks, which would place their birth sometime around Easter.)

I marveled at the slender pup's speed and wildness, imagining what it must have been like for that little wild thing to leap from the back porch down into that brambly thicket. A little sadly, I turned and went back to my truck, to the other pup still waiting by the roadside.

No matter, I told myself; *a pup wild as that slender one—more of a coyote, really—wouldn't have made a very good pet anyway.*

I got in the truck with the heavy pup, who wagged her tail and blinked her long eyelashes at me, ecstatic, and I drove on down the road.

With what subtle assuagements does landscape sculpt our hearts, our emotions; and from that catalyst, sometimes, our actions? I followed the winding road through the dusk tunnel of soft green light, and as I passed by the same place, a couple hundred yards down the road, where I'd first felt the impulse to turn around and go back for the pups, I felt it again. It was a feeling, a change, as dramatic as if I had passed through a doorway, and into an entirely different room. *You know,* I thought, *I ought not to split those little pups up like that.*

I turned around at about the same spot in the road and went back to give it one more try.

When I pulled back up to the abandoned house, the slender pup, Homer, was sitting out on the side of the road, in the same place where she had been earlier. I stopped the truck and jumped out, at which point she whirled and bolted, scampered up the viny trail and right back into the dark, old falling-down house. I hurried after her, and once more went from room to room, looking for a tiny, frightened wild pup, but found nothing, only decay. And once more I came finally to the back porch, with its storm-sprung doorless frame yawing straight into the gloom of jungle beyond.

What a pup, I marveled. *What a wild thing, making that four-foot leap into thorn and bramble. Too wild*, I thought again sadly, though my sorrow was tempered by the pleasure of having salvaged the one sweet little pup, and I returned to the truck knowing somehow that she would make a wonderful pet for someone; and, as before, she was thrilled to see me: thrilled to be petted, belly-thumped, noticed. Not yet loved, but noticed.

It was just before dark. I drove on down the road; and, amazingly, as I passed through that same invisible curtain—a curve of landscape, a mosaic of forest, and an open field beyond—I had the same feeling I'd had both times before. *There's still just a little bit of light left; I ought to try one more time. I ought to use up that last little bit of light trying.*

I turned around and went back to the old house. And again, the little hound was perched out front, on the roadside.

This time when she saw my truck she whirled and ran for the house even before I'd stopped; but I was quick, this time, and leapt from my truck and crossed the road in long strides, and hurdled the sagging, rusted iron gate, and plowed through the brambles, gaining on the pup.

She scampered up the steps and into the house. I was close behind, and this time I went straight to the back, hoping to catch her before she made that amazing leap.

But not quite. I was just a little too late, for when I came to that blasted-out doorway, again there was nothing but space, emptiness, and jungle beyond. The evening's first fireflies were beginning to cruise, as if sealing over the space into which the little hound had leapt, in the same manner with which the rings on a pond settle out to flatness, sealing over a stone that has been tossed into the pond's center.

Foiled again, and feeling a little foolish, a little defeated, and anxious to get on over to Elizabeth's before it got too late, I turned back to my truck, and to the one waiting puppy, again.

I was halfway down the hallway—the disintegrating shack eerie, ominous, in the failing light—when a new thought occurred to me: as if it had taken a shift in lighting to shove away an old assumption, and yield—tentatively, cautiously, at first—a new perspective.

That back-porch leap would be a heck of a jump for an animal as small as that pup to make; and to be making it again and again, so relentlessly—well, wasn't that a bit much? And how was she getting all the way out to the front of the house again so quickly, each time, after being swallowed by the jungle?

In all my previous explorations, I'd only glanced in each room. There was only the dullest blue light remaining, here and there, in the house. Dusk's first stars were visible through the cracks and rips in the roof. Owls were calling.

I went from room to room, checking behind the old moldering cardboard boxes of pots and pans, and rotting clothes, and mildewed ancient magazines, fast on their way to becoming humus. In each room, nothing, until I got to the last room—a wild clutter of yellowing newspapers—where I noticed what I had not before, a littering of small, dried-out twists of dog dung. As if they had been living in this room for quite some time.

There was a pile of loose sheets of newspaper over in the far corner of the room, by the window, and in the dim light, I could see that the papers were rattling slightly, as if from a breeze. I stepped over to the corner and lifted the sheets of paper, and there she was—tinier than I had remembered; and no longer fierce or barksome; and no longer any superdog, capable of great and daring leaps of escape; but instead a quivering, terrified little pup.

She was warm when I picked her up, and this time she did not resist. I tucked her in against my body and carried her out into the night to rejoin her sister.

Cows were lowing in the fields, a summer sound, when I arrived at Elizabeth's farmhouse. Steam was drifting in from off the bayou.

"What are you going to do with them?" Elizabeth asked.

"Oh, I'll take them to the animal rescue league tomorrow," I said—never dreaming or imagining otherwise—though a short time later, as we watched them crouch bowlegged in front of a pan of milk and gulp at it until their bellies were stretched thumping tight, their tails wagging, it must have occurred to me, just the faintest shadow of a thought at first, *Well, I guess I could wait a day or two. . . .*

Homer was named for a character in a novel that I was read-ing at the time. There was something about her slender elegance, even in her temporary disarray—patchy fur, burrs, etc.—that told me she was feminine enough to carry such a name, and to turn it from the masculine to the feminine.

Ann was named for Orphan Annie.

They slept in a cardboard box together—under a thin sheet, their heads tucked against each other's shoulders. They slept soundly, not whining at all the way most pups do, but snoring slightly—as if completely content, now that they had finally gotten to where they needed to be. Having given them a little milk, and assigned them names, how could I turn them away?

I held them, tiny in my hands. I followed them as if through a door, and nothing was ever the same. By stopping four, five minutes and picking up those sweet, funny, vulnera-ble little hounds, I stepped off the train tracks of my old life and into a slightly different world, where I stood at peace at the edge of shadows and sun dapple.

When we moved to Montana the dogs were depressed at first, missing Mississippi; they lay by the back door of the cabin for a solid month. But they grew accustomed to the new country and fell in love with life again. They went for hikes with me, chased the coyotes out of the yard, learned the new scents, new routines. They became mountain dogs soon enough; they refashioned themselves, out of loyalty. They learned about snow, about the values of a spot by the fireplace on a cold evening and the glories of muddy spring. They learned how certain things were backwards here, such as the geese leaving in the autumn, rather than arriving.

What else was there to do but adjust, and to love life?

I would often observe their loyalty, and watch their pleasure in this new place in the world, and try, in some units of measurement not yet known to man, to quantify the distance they had come, from being at death's door in Mississippi to chewing on a moldering old elk skull outside the cabin in Montana.

And I realized, soon enough, that that distance for them was the same distance for me.

Welcome to Newark Airport

Jon Katz

He was a two-year-old Border collie of Australian lineage, well-bred but high-strung, and in big trouble. He had been shown at obedience trials in the Southwest. But something had gone very wrong with this arrangement and his breeder had taken him back and was working to find him a home. He needed one badly, she told me. That was all I knew about Devon when I drove to Newark Airport to pick him up.

I already had two sweet dogs and I had plenty of non-dog-related responsibilities as well. I wasn't particularly keen on taking in a third dog.

But this breeder, who kept a fierce eye on her dogs even after they'd left her kennels, had been e-mailing me for a while. She'd read a book of mine called *Running to the Mountain*, which featured Julius and Stanley, not only as cover dogs but as major characters.

She called me up; before long we were spending hours on the phone. Deanne wasn't pushing me, she kept saying, but she believed this dog belonged with me.

I'd been fascinated by Border collies for years, poring over books, browsing websites where owners post stories of their dogs' weird behavior, exchanging tentative e-mails with breeders. They were such intelligent dogs, I'd read, and somehow exotic. But everyone I consulted said more or less the same thing: unless you have a hundred acres right outside your back door, don't do it. I had only a normal suburban New Jersey yard—and did I mention that I already had two large dogs?

So I hemmed and hawed about adopting a Border collie, especially one with more than the usual . . . issues. A part of me was drawn to the idea, but the rational part said: Stop! Danger ahead!

Deanne was patient, persuasive, persistent without being pushy, a subtle line she walked with great skill. The better we got to know each other, the more effective her message. Devon, she said, was a special case in need of special handling. He was uncommonly bright, willful, and emotionally beat-up. From my book, with its descriptions of Julius and Stanley and of my cabin in rural upstate New York—close to Border collie nirvana—she suspected that I had a high tolerance for odd dog behavior. And Devon was, well, odd.

After a few weeks of this back-and-forth, she put him on a plane and shipped him from Lubbock, Texas, eastward to his new life. On a balmy spring night, I stood outside the American Airlines baggage freight window in Terminal B.

Waiting nervously, I recalled in particular the warning of breeder and author Janet Larson. She was straightforward: "In Border collies, the wild type or wolf temperament is common and seems to be genetically linked to the herding behavior. This means that many Border collies make unstable pets, and some can be dangerous. Remember that these dogs were developed as sheepherders, and in the mountains and moors they did not need to be sociable with strangers. As a result, shy and sharp temperaments are fairly common."

In my thickly settled neighborhood only about fifteen miles west of New York City, you don't encounter many mountains or moors. You don't see many Border collies, either.

Doing my homework had only increased my trepidation. Border collies need vast spaces to roam, I read. They had insatiable energy; they'd go nuts living out the fate of many suburban family hounds: locked in crates all day while the grownups worked; never properly trained, socialized, or exercised; growing increasingly neurotic while the kids, for whose sake the dogs were allegedly acquired, often wound up ignoring them.

Border collies, I read further, sometimes mistook kids for sheep and nipped or bit them. They had peculiar habits, interests, needs and mood swings. Working dogs in every sense of the word, diggers and foragers, they abhorred loneliness and inactivity and hated having nothing to do. If you didn't give them something to keep them occupied, they would find something themselves.

They often had trouble with other dogs, herding or chasing them. They obsessively pursued squirrels, rabbits, chipmunks, cars, and trucks—that is to say, anything that moved quickly away from them. Always in pursuit of something mobile, they'd take off explosively when they found it, racing after it at blinding speeds. Once launched, few things—shrubbery, fences, traffic, shouts—could slow them down.

Newark Airport is a sometimes overwhelming place, justly famous for its nearly continual mobs, traffic, congestion, and delays. Devon's plane had been routed through Atlanta, and the airport monitors said that his flight would be late. This had to be rough on any dog, let alone a wired-up Border collie with a delicate psychological history. Poor guy. I pictured him in the dark hold, feeling the plane move, the crates and luggage vibrating as the deafening engine roared nearby. Terminal B was unlikely to be a welcoming destination, either.

I had only the vaguest sense of what this dog looked like. I'd declined Deanne's offer of a photograph, mostly because I didn't want to make an adoption decision based on looks. That was a bad reason, I thought, to get a dog.

Parts of his story were vague. He had never lived in a house much or, I gathered, had a single human to attach himself to. He'd been neutered only a couple of weeks earlier, by the owner, before she gave him back to Deanne. The usually routine surgery had gone badly: the vets couldn't put him to sleep with the usual amount of anesthesia, so they increased the dosage, and then they almost couldn't wake him up. He was iron willed and smart.

"Devon's got some things to deal with," Deanne told me. My understanding was that Devon had been raised for obedience competition, had fallen short in some way, and had been replaced. This wasn't an uncommon fate in obedience show dogs, who aren't raised to be pets. When they fail—and they know when they fail—they have no real purpose.

So Devon had languished. "He needs somebody to connect to," Deanne told me. "He's discouraged." She also told me I could change his name—it was a tad [pretentious] for my taste—but I figured he'd have enough to adjust to.

Border collie breeders are notoriously picky, since so many of their weird and energetic animals wind up abandoned or unwanted. I suspect they tend to look either for ranchers with hordes of sheep or stay-at-home oddballs—writers, for example—to take in the rejects.

It seemed that when I'd mentioned—during the interminable interviewing any potential Border collie owner is subjected to—that Stanley liked to give my butt a nibble when he wanted me to throw his ball, that clinched something for Deanne. You had to have an unusual sense of humor, she said, to appreciate Border collies. So Devon was en route. I'm still not entirely sure why I agreed.

What would this do to Julius and Stanley, who had placid dog lives filled with chew bones, stuffed toy animals, strolls to the park, and regular retreats upstate, where Stanley loved to swim while Julius stared happily at the mountaintop at nothing in particular for hours? They enjoyed the finest hypoallergenic light dog food; summer vacations on Cape Cod; four, sometimes five walks a day and round-the-clock companionship with each other. They'd returned these favors with nothing but love and loyalty.

I had left them in the yard that night, where they could meet Devon. Given a bit of space, perhaps nobody would get territorial or testy.

"Boys," I'd announced solemnly, "I'm bringing another dog here, Devon. He might be a little wacky. Be patient." Julius and Stanley looked at me fondly, both tails wagging. They were nothing if not patient.

I had put a bowl and a jug of water in my minivan, along with a small bag of biscuits. I was holding a new blue leash and collar, to which I'd already attached a dog tag with Devon's name and my phone numbers.

I felt anxious, dubious, excited, strongly pulled toward something that made no sense. It was not much comfort to hear that Deanne had promised I could send the dog back to her if he couldn't adapt.

An hour after I arrived, the plane landed. Pacing nervously outside the freight office, I asked every five minutes or so if a dog was on board. I called Deanne on my cell phone to tell her that Devon had arrived. I called my wife, Paula, for reassurance; convinced that three dogs was at least one too many, she didn't offer much. I called my daughter at college. "He's almost here," I announced. She sighed a familiar sigh. "Call back and let me know what he's like."

A half-hour after touchdown—it was by now nine P.M.—I saw two baggage handlers pulling a large blue dog crate, dragging and bumping it noisily across the tiled floor. The plastic container was enormous, with air holes along the sides, and a metal grill over the front opening. An envelope taped on top held the dog's travel and AKC papers. A blanket, the only vestige of his former life, was scrunched up against the door, along with an empty bowl, and shredded bits of newspaper lined the bottom.

I couldn't see much through the front grill, just flashes of black and white that seemed to circle frantically, like a pinwheel. He was throwing himself against the door and the sides. I winced at the loud bumping; he needed to get out of there.

They pulled the crate alongside me. "Hey Devon," I said to the plastic. No response.

I presented the required ID, signed the freight bill, and pulled the crate to a part of the baggage area where there was a bit of room.

Newark airport, almost always bedlam, was worse than usual that night because of bad-weather delays all over the East. Luggage was piled everywhere; cops screamed at idling drivers through the open doors; skycaps yelled for business; and the loudspeaker rattled off one flight after another as the jets roared overhead. Thousands of people poured through the doors and along the concourses.

My van was parked a few hundred yards from the door. My plan was to reach into the crate and leash Devon, then walk him with one hand while I toted the crate in the other; we'd get away from this madness and save our bonding for the quieter, darker parking lot. Section 3A of the Terminal B short-term parking area didn't exactly conjure up pastoral scenes from James Herriot, but it would have to do.

Inside the crate, Devon was still pinwheeling. I'd yet to glimpse his face.

"Devon," I called. "Devon, I'm going to open the door,

boy. It's going to be okay." I've always talked to my dogs, not because I imagine they understand my words, but so that they can pick up my tone or mood. It's almost a reflex.

The thumping and twirling stopped, and I saw a pair of wild, ink-dark eyes. They bespoke power and intensity, as well as terror. And no wonder. In the morning, home, in laid-back, sparsely populated Texas. Then to the airport, into a crate, onto a plane's cargo hold. Takeoffs and landings, not once but twice. Holed up in the dark. Hours in the air. Unloaded down a ramp, driven across the airport's dank runways, dragged across the floor of a tumultuous terminal, confronted with a large stranger calling his name.

I knelt, pulled up the latch on the crate, and the gate slammed open into my face. Before I could move, a blur shot past me and into the crowd, its force knocking me off my heels onto my back. Devon was out of sight before I could scramble to my feet. A flurry of shrieks and shouts behind me told which way he'd headed.

It took me, two baggage handlers, and three very unhappy Port Authority police officers nearly half an hour to track and corral Devon as he ricocheted through the jammed terminal, scaring travelers out of their wits as he dashed in panic. He had no bearings, no reference points or instincts but flight.

The Port Authority officers were not dog lovers, it turned out. "Hey, he's a champion Border collie," I pleaded as one got on his radio to alert Newark's animal-control team.

"We aren't dogcatchers," he said. But he wasn't totally

unsympathetic either, and they agreed that we would try to restrain Devon before calling in the doggie SWAT unit. They warned, however, that they wouldn't be held responsible if he nipped some kid, or if an old woman got knocked over. "I've seen dogs a lot less excited than that one bite people," one muttered.

Any mishaps would be on my head. And the officer wasn't wrong. A panicked dog in a strange place could be dangerous. What if someone grabbed him? But the thought of Devon locked up in a shelter made my stomach drop. So we set off after him.

He sprinted from one baggage carousel to another, then back again. He seemed to be desperately looking for some running room, or perhaps a familiar sight. He couldn't find either.

Whenever we'd get close, he'd turn and bolt, vanishing into the crowds. My nightmare was that he'd dash out one of the doorways into the vast parking lots, which stretched out forever, bounded by teeming highways. Devon could easily get hit—or if he made it through, he might disappear into the acres of meadows, refineries, truck bays, and warehouses that surround the airport. I shouted his name. It didn't slow him a whit.

Occasionally, he'd wheel back toward us. A few brave and sympathetic travelers even called out and reached for him, but he turned, barked, and snarled. Parents grabbed their kids. The cops had lost patience.

But eventually we seemed to have driven him more or less into a corner near a Hertz counter, a cop on either side behind me. I was out front, moving slowly toward him.

I knelt in front of him, leaving a few yards between us. It was my first good look at him. Devon was a beautiful creature, sleek and black with a needle nose, a narrow white blaze on his forehead, a white chest. He was skinny, his fur matted, and he was hunched over after hours in the crate. I could see pale stains along his face, probably from panicky spittle during the trip. His eyes were inexpressibly deep, enchanting, and sad.

He was panting heavily, spent and frightened, probably dehydrated. I had to get him under control, or he'd end up in a Port Authority kennel or, worse, loping along a highway.

Eye contact was critical with Border collies. All the books said so; it was the way they dominated livestock. Perhaps Devon would respond. At the least, a moment's pause in his race might give me a chance to grab him. I could see him gauging the distance between me, the officers to my rear and a small crowd of people, whom I suspected were concerned dog types, forming a raggedy semicircle behind the police.

He was an obedience dog, supposedly. "Devon. Stay. Devon. Stay," I kept repeating, a quiet chant. "I'm your new friend. I'm the guy. It's okay now. It's okay. Stay. We're going to go home." I kept my voice soothing and even, hoping the repetition would calm him. I was panting, too, and sweating.

I pulled a dog biscuit out of my pants pocket. His darting eyes focused on me, then glanced at the biscuit. I put it on the ground and nudged it toward him. He ignored it, looking almost disdainful. Could I possibly think he could be bought off that cheaply? He seemed offended.

And I could see him calculating, calculating, calculating.

Can I run for it? Can I get past this jerk and all these people? A baggage carousel sputtering into motion caught his eye for a moment. Was that a possible escape route? Then, as if he'd suddenly grown resigned, his posture relaxed a bit. Maybe he had figured out that the terminal led nowhere he wanted to go. I inched forward on my knees slowly, talking quietly, feeling like a hostage negotiator. This was now a major scene. My anxiety was enhanced by acute embarrassment.

"Stay," I said, raising my palm, firming my voice. "Stay, Devon. It's okay." He seemed mildly amused now, and began concentrating on me, taking me in, pondering my technique, tilting his head curiously as I gestured. He was definitely listening to me, sizing me up.

I got closer, close enough to reach behind his ear and scratch him gently. He let me. The cops began to back away. Then some kid shouted, and Devon started, looking wild again. But I scratched him again, and patted his shoulders. I felt for his collar and slipped the leash onto the metal ring. He didn't resist or run, he just kept staring at me.

The leash seemed to settle him down, as if he finally understood what he was supposed to do, which was to go with me. The officers, muttering, looked relieved and went off to do something more important. At least nobody had been bitten or hurt.

By now, a number of people in the crowd were murmuring about how beautiful Devon was, clucking sympathetically when I loudly announced that he'd come all the way from Texas, that this was his first time on a plane, the first time he'd met me. And he was beautiful, this dervish who weighed, I guessed, somewhere between forty and fifty pounds.

I held the leash on my left, and Devon walked along hesitantly as I pulled the crate behind us. He wanted nothing to do with it. "Heel," I tried, to no particular effect. But he wasn't trying to escape. For the moment, I was all he had.

We walked outside past the rows and rows of cars until we reached the van. At first he lurched one way, then the other, then settled into trotting along beside me, turning as I did, the mark of a trained dog. Maybe I just didn't know the right commands.

I unlocked the van's rear door, pushed in the huge crate, then came around to the side, still holding the leash. A powerful curiosity was taking over a bit from the terror. Devon was noticing everything, reacting to every sound, to the lights, buses, and people. His eyes seemed astonishingly expressive and alert.

I pulled out the jug and bowl and poured him some water. He slurped it up greedily. Then I crouched next to him on the pavement. It was a surreal encounter in the ugly yellow safety light, with cars pouring past us in a stream, but Devon didn't shy away. I handed him another biscuit, which he inhaled. Then two more.

I reached over slowly and scratched the top of his head; his ears came up for the first time. Every thirty seconds or so, a jet would blast overhead and Devon would shake a bit, but after two or three takeoffs, he got used to it.

"Devon, listen to me, pal," I said, trying again. "It's going to be okay." He gazed up at me, and at the sky above us, and looked utterly lost and defeated. I kept scratching him and handing over biscuits, which he kept eating. He was making up his mind about me, as I was about him.

"Look, we're going to get into the car now. We're going to go home," I told him. "I don't know what you've been through, but I work at home, I'll stay with you, I'll give you lots of walks, lots of food, lots of patience. I'll take good care of you. Let's try it, okay?" I held out my hand, and he licked it, once, very gently.

I opened the door and Devon jumped up onto the front seat as if he'd done it a million times. I lowered the front window a bit—he stuck his nose out. Curiosity was my ally here; from inside the van, the airport was more fascinating than terrifying—though when we got to the parking-lot cashier's booth, he jumped onto the floor and hid.

Then he jumped back up, looking at me, then out the window. The wheels were turning: *Who is this guy? What is this place? Where are we going?*

"It's okay," I kept saying. "It's all right." Sometimes he appeared to believe me.

Fifteen minutes later, we pulled into my driveway. The Labs came lumbering over to the fence, tails wagging. Devon's head went down, his ears folded, and the three touched noses cautiously. Julius looked at me with regret and concern. Stanley, the slightly more dominant of the two, looked skeptical.

I decided to take Devon for a short walk before introducing him to Paula and the house. Partway down the block, he was walking alongside me so easily, his nose to the ground sniffing the pavement, that I relaxed a bit for the first time that night. My tree-lined suburban street seemed serene compared to Newark Airport.

An ill-advised reverie: with a sharp jerk of the leash from my hand, Devon was gone. I spun around in all directions and saw no trace of him—until I happened to glance at a passing minivan and saw him perched on the roof as it drove slowly down the street. I didn't believe it. I *couldn't* believe it. Dogs don't fly.

Brandishing a pooper-scooper in my right hand, I gave chase, shouting as I went, "Hey! Hey, stop! Stop, there's a dog on the car." My neighbors walking their terrier across the street paused in shock and stared.

The van slowed, a trusting act by a driver who'd probably looked in his rearview mirror to see what the tumult was about. Who knows what he or she thought at the sight of a 230-pound man galumphing down the street, waving a strange device and screaming. The van began to speed up.

How did he get up there?

I stopped and shouted as loudly as I ever have, "Devon, come! Now!" My voice wasn't pleading, but angry. Perhaps thirty yards down the street, he hopped off as nimbly as if the van were a small step stool and lighted on the sidewalk.

"Sit!" I screamed. He did, looking up at me in some bewilderment, perhaps wondering why I was making so much noise. Then he averted his face, as if in shame or fear that I would strike him. He remained absolutely still as I grabbed his leash, and we headed back to the house.

My dog year had begun.

Cody, Come Home!

Petina Barrett

T ired of playing in the house, my five-year-old son, Cody, and his friend Justin tromped noisily downstairs. "Can I go over to Justin's?" Cody asked.

"Just remember to call me as soon as you get there," I said. Cody nodded and followed Justin outside. "Don't forget!" I called after them. From the living room window, I watched the boys head down the driveway together. Nearby, at the edge of the woods, a scruffy dog sniffed the grass before taking off into the trees. *That's the second stray this week. I'm glad Cody didn't see it,* I thought. We often came across lost dogs in our rural neighborhood. "Where's his family?" Cody would always ask.

"We'll take him to the Humane Society," I'd say. "They'll make sure he gets home okay." That wasn't really a lie. The Humane Society worked hard to find good homes for all the dogs we found. The lucky ones had just slipped off their leashes and were soon reunited with the people who loved them. I couldn't tell Cody that some of these dogs had probably been abandoned. He looked to me to make everything right with the world, like when he was frightened by a loud noise and ran to me for protection. It would scare him to think of a dog wandering lost in the dark woods all alone.

Maybe one day we'll adopt a dog ourselves, I thought as I went to the laundry room to unload the dryer. *That would be at least one dog taken care of.* I folded the last of Cody's T-shirts and glanced up at the clock. Fifteen minutes had passed. *Oh, Cody,* I sighed.

I grabbed the phone. I'd just finished dialing when thunder cracked overhead. Stepping into the living room, I saw the sky was now steely gray. Rain washed down in sheets and slapped against the windows. "Hello?" said Justin's father on the phone. I couldn't ask fast enough. "Did the boys get there okay?" I said, hoping Cody was not too upset by the thunder.

"Justin came in about ten minutes ago," his dad said. "He says Cody went home through the woods." I could barely see the trees through the downpour. *Cody must still be out there.* I imagined him huddled by a bush somewhere, scared and alone, just like those strays. "I'll find him," I said, hanging up. *Lord, we try to help those dogs find their way home. Please help Cody find his.*

I grabbed my raincoat, ran to the front door and stopped short. Through the window I saw my son coming up the drive with a huge, shaggy yellow dog lumbering alongside him.

"Cody!" I called, running out to meet them. They were soaked through and through. The dog trotted up to the house with us. "Stay," Cody said. The dog obediently sat down on the porch. I ran inside to get a towel and dried Cody off in the entryway. The dog watched us through the window, never taking his eyes off Cody. "I was so worried," I said, "thinking about you all alone out there."

"The thunder was scary," Cody said as I tousled his hair with the towel. "But that big dog came and found me so I wasn't scared anymore. I named him Gabriel."

The dog pricked up his ears. "Well, he sure seems to know his name," I laughed. "You run and get some dry clothes while I fetch Gabriel some food." I went to the kitchen. *If Gabriel's a stray*, I thought as I put some cold cuts in a bowl, *then he's just found himself a home!* Every boy needed a guardian angel, after all. But when I stepped out on the porch the dog was gone. "Gabriel!" I called. The rain had stopped, and Cody and I looked around the yard. "I guess he just disappeared," I said finally.

Cody nodded. "God probably sent him to help someone else."

I looked into the woods. We couldn't take care of every lost creature. But that's where God—and all his guardian angels—come in. Rain or shine.

An Angel of a Dog

Lois Spoon

When I found a marble-size lump in my breast, I tried to tell myself it was nothing. I was forty-two and had enjoyed good health my whole life. But deep down I knew better: My mother had died from breast cancer, which meant I was high-risk.

Finally I summoned my courage and called the doctor. A mammogram and a biopsy confirmed my worst fear. The lump was malignant and doctors advised a radical double mastectomy. I agreed to have the surgery. And although my medical questions were answered, and my husband and son gave me endless love and support, I kept a lot of my worries to myself. I wished for another woman to talk to. Someone who understood completely what I was going through. *Lord, help me through this.*

Only days after the four-hour surgery I was released from the hospital, but I still seemed to spend more time with doctors and nurses and counselors than I did at home. I went to physical therapy every day, but rehabilitation was slow. Simple things such as rolling down a car window or opening a jar of peanut butter had become painstaking tasks.

Then at a follow-up visit with my oncologist I got even worse news. The cancer had spread far into my lymphatic system. "Frankly, Lois, we can't be optimistic about the prognosis," the doctor said, unable to cushion the blow. Even with chemotherapy, the odds of my surviving were small.

Back home I sank onto a chair and watched the rain through the window. I had never felt so completely alone.

I got up to draw the curtains when I noticed a Siberian husky trotting up the walk as if he knew just where he was going. I'd never seen him before. I went over to the window. The dog cocked his head slightly and studied me. He came closer to the window and I saw he had one blue eye and one brown. For a few moments he stared, then went to sniff around the front yard.

Wait a minute, I thought. *What did I just read about a missing husky?* I grabbed the previous day's paper and thumbed to the lost-and-found section. There it was—a description of a lost dog exactly like this one. I dialed the number listed. A woman answered. "I think your dog is in my yard," I told her.

"I can't believe it," she said. "Wolfy's been missing for weeks! Please give me your address. I'll be right over."

I went back to the window. How could I make sure the dog would stay until his owner came for him? Robert and Luke were out, and I couldn't restrain the big animal on my own.

Sitting back down, I tried to keep an eye on the dog as he wandered around the yard. In about ten minutes a knock came at the door. "I'm Becky," the woman said. "Where's my Wolfy?"

"You don't see him in the yard?" I looked for him myself. "Oh, no! He was here just a second ago."

"I'll check around the neighborhood," she said. "He couldn't have gone far."

The woman returned about twenty minutes later. "Well, he's managed to disappear again," she said. "But I'm grateful you called me."

I felt awful for Becky. That, on top of my own problems, got me dabbing my eyes with a tissue.

"Are you okay?" Becky asked.

"Yes," I said. But she persisted.

"You sure?"

All of a sudden a gush of tears poured from my eyes.

"Let's talk about it," Becky said, patting my arm. Something told me it was okay and I invited her in. "My name's Lois," I said. We sat on the sofa, and I explained what was happening to me. When I finished she put her arms around me.

"Lois, I want to tell you something," she said. "Four years ago I had the exact same diagnosis and the exact same prognosis. Just like you I was given little hope for survival. But here I am. It can happen to you too," she said. "God will stand by you every step of the way—and so will I."

That day I gained immeasurable strength from Becky. I confided all my deepest fears to her, and it made me feel better when she said, "I know what you mean. That's how I felt too." She became a wonderful friend, always knowing just the right words to encourage me when I didn't think I could stand another round of chemo. Sad to say, though, she never did find Wolfy—God had other plans for him.

It's been six years since my surgery. I beat the odds. With Becky in my corner, I'm not surprised. I think it's safe to say that a dog only heaven could have sent wanted me to meet her.

Lessons Learned

from a Dog

Puppy Club

Nancy Long Tafoya

I clipped the leash onto Buster's collar and opened the front door. So many times we'd headed out together like this to visit my dad at his nursing home. But with Dad's recent death, I'd also lost a big part of my day-to-day life. No more calling to consult with the nurses, no more looking after his financial affairs, no more finding just the right card to send him. To make matters worse, two of my best friends had moved away. I suddenly found I had a lot of time to myself, time to ponder the aloneness of being without Dad. *God*, I prayed, *send me some new friends for this new phase of my life*.

Buster bounded out into the brisk September dusk. "You're great, boy," I said, reaching down to stroke his wiry fur, "but I wouldn't mind having some more human companions too." My husband, Al, and I don't have children, so we lavish lots of attention on our one-year-old Border terrier. I look forward to my evening walks with Buster. Sometimes he leads me across the street from our apartment to visit the New York Dog Spa & Hotel, where he'd had his obedience training. But that evening he headed toward a resale clothing shop, where a small tricolor spaniel peered through the front door. Buster put his paw on the glass, then looked up at me.

A young woman with long brown hair opened the door. "Hi, I'm Terin," she said. "Maybe your dog will get along with my Max." The animals sniffed at each other, then launched into a wild chase amid the racks of clothes. "This is Jennifer," said Terin, pointing to a blond woman behind the counter. She was laughing at the dogs' antics. "And here's Baci and Robin," Terin said, opening the door again.

In came a tall woman and a rotund black pug, who joined in Buster and Max's chase. "Wow, Baci hardly ever plays like that," said Robin. "He's got a problem with his legs."

"Looks like Buster's a good influence," Terin said when she closed the shop a half hour later. "Why don't you bring him back to visit sometime?"

In fact, it was Buster who brought me back to the store again and again. I usually sat quietly on the couch in the middle of the store and watched him romp with Max and Baci. Terin, Robin and Jennifer seemed to have the same kind of fun, easy time together. *I wish I could be more like you, Buster,* I thought. *Then maybe I could join in too.* But that didn't seem likely. I was old enough to be Jennifer's mother. Plus, they were all single and I'd been married forever.

One thing we did have in common was our devotion to our dogs. Max refereed when Buster and Baci wrestled. Baci's legs grew strong enough for him to jump up on the couch. We spent hours swapping stories about our "boys."

Slowly, I started to open up about myself as well. One day I read Jennifer a prayer I'd written about losing my father; she hugged me, tears in her eyes. Another time, Terin confided she was having problems with the man she was dating, and I gave her my best big-sister advice.

Finally I took the next step. "Buster would like Max and Baci to come over for dinner," I announced to the girls. We made plans to get together.

The evening was a hit. The dining table was festooned with new dog toys and small, framed pictures of Buster for our guests to take home.

The next night at the store, Robin said to me, "I told my grandmother about Buster's party. She can't believe what my friends and I do for our dogs!"

My *friends*. It was amazing. Within a very short period of time, I had made three new friends. And then I remembered my prayer. When I'm able to visualize something and ask for God's help, it often comes to be.

As we went out to the street later, I reached down to pet my puppy. "Thanks, Buster," I said. He had taught me to be more open—both to new people and to God working through all his creatures to give us just what we need.

When Daddy Decided to Splurge

Roberta L. Messner

A friend was going to look after my dog, Muffin, while I went into the hospital for some surgery. On the way to her house I stopped to see my mom and dad, Muffin trotting in after me as though she were a regular member of the family. A Benji look-alike, she'd been my soul mate for seven years. From the first time I'd spotted the wiry-haired stray hiding in the briers by a chainlink fence, we'd been inseparable. I'd always tried to give her the best life I could.

"Muffin will be just fine while you're gone," Mom assured me.

"I can't believe you're not putting that mongrel up at the Hilton," Dad commented. "The way you spoil her! Giving her that fancy-dancy stocking full of dog biscuits at Christmastime and taking her everywhere."

I steeled myself against his words. That I spent too much money on Muffin was an old issue. That I should be saving for a rainy day was an even older argument.

"I've always told myself," Dad went on, "that I'd be better off if I were Roberta's dog."

I just hugged Muffin a little harder and tried to ignore

Dad's remarks. But even after I left, they stung. I dropped Muffin off at my friend's and drove on to the hospital, still thinking of what Dad had said. Why did his criticism hurt so much? I was a grown woman with a successful career as a nurse. Why did his approval matter? It was as though I were a little girl again, trying to make my daddy proud.

A child of the Depression, Dad had had to be careful with money. He'd worked as a telegraph operator on the railroad and supplemented his earnings selling old pocket watches at flea markets. A horse trader, people called him. When I was barely out of diapers, I picked up his jargon. He loved to tell about the time he tugged on my pigtails and asked if I'd take a five-dollar bill for my Tiny Tears doll. I took a long look at her pink bottle and packet of tissues and shot back, "I want more, this here's a rare one!"

By the time I was ten years old, I was doing odd jobs in the neighborhood, hoping to match Dad's industry. I hosed off porch furniture, waxed floors, and starched the curtains in a neighbor's guest bedroom.

With the first dollar I earned, I put aside ten percent for church, but the next ten cents I took straight to Broughton's Dairy. There I bought a double-dip cone of lime sherbet, Daddy's favorite, and climbed the steep iron stairs of the telegraph tower where he worked.

I tapped on the screen door and hollered, "Surprise!" I just knew he'd be pleased. "I bought this for you with the money I've been making." Lime-green sherbet dripped down my fingers as Daddy tapped out a Morse code message.

Finally he looked up and smiled. But as he took a lick of soupy sherbet, he cautioned, "Don't be squandering all your hard-earned money on ice cream now. You should be putting something away for the future."

All the way home I fought back tears. Wasn't there anything I could do to make him happy? When I was a little older I took up the violin so I could join in when he pulled out his fiddle. Then I studied piano. My first recital, I knew how proud he'd be of the way I played "The Londonderry Air." But at the last minute Daddy couldn't come. He had to work overtime. We needed the money. For a rainy day.

After I studied nursing and pursued my RN career, I became something of a horse trader myself, going to flea markets, collecting antiques. No matter what I bought, Dad was able to take the wind out of my sails when I told him the deal I'd made or how much I'd managed to save.

With Muffin, though, I never cut corners. She deserved the very best. In the hospital after my surgery, I kept thinking of how happy I'd be to see her again.

It was then that I received word Muffin had jumped the fence in my friend's backyard and raced off. No one could find her. Lying in my hospital bed, I prayed that whatever happened, she would be safe. Still, when no news came, I was frantic.

The morning my mother drove me home from the hospital, all I saw were dogs. Dogs playing, dogs barking, dogs running to greet their masters. But no wagging tail awaited me when I got home.

"I'm so sorry, Roberta," Mom said, tucking a blanket around me on the sofa. "Your father is worried too."

Yeah, right, I thought, scrunching miserably into the pillow. Later, I got up to make a cup of tea, and the phone rang. The caller said she'd seen the ad about Muffin and wanted me to know she'd just lost her little pooch and knew exactly how I felt.

The ad? I wondered groggily before stumbling back to rest.

The next night I got more calls. One man who worked at the Waffle House asked for a better description of Muffin. Before hanging up he added, "Your dad must think the world of you to go to all this trouble." *Why did he say that?* Another caller said, "The dog your father described to me is here, I'm sure of it." *What were they talking about?*

The following day a coworker drove me around to check on the leads I'd received. None of the shaggy mutts people had found were Muffin. One was a hundred miles away, but I knew how Muffin loved to jump into any open car door, so I felt compelled to investigate. Alas, the "female dog with matted hair" turned out to be a male cat. "I felt so bad for you I guess I got carried away," the stranger admitted.

Then my sister called. "I found Muffin at the pound!" I was beside myself with relief as I went with her to investigate. But I knew at once when I approached the cage that the thin, mangy dog wasn't my Muffin.

"Just call her name," my sister urged. "Maybe she's lost weight."

"Muffin!" I cried. And from the saddest corridor in the animal world, fifty-six dogs of every description howled in unison.

With that my heart just broke. All those animals longing for a home expressed my own longing for my dog. It was as though my loneliness had found a voice.

That night another stranger called. She wanted me to know she was praying for me. "I don't know why this had to happen to you, honey," she said, "but God knows how you feel. Trust him with your sadness."

By then I had given up, but when one more person called, absolutely certain he had my dog, I allowed myself to hope one more time. A friend drove me to the end of a muddy hollow, where a man stood with a yelping, stubby-tailed orange dog much bigger than Muffin. "She just has to be yours," he insisted as the huge dog pawed my skirt.

"I don't think so," I said sadly.

The man looked at me woefully. "Lady," he said, "I've already promised my grandkids a trip to Disney World with all that reward money your father's giving."

I was stunned. "Reward?" From the man who always accused me of squandering money on Muffin? The thrifty father who wanted me to save for a rainy day?

"I got the ad right here." He pulled out the beat-up newspaper he had jammed in his back pocket. "See, this one." He held out the want ads and pointed to an item he'd circled.

I took the paper, read it once, then twice, blinking hard to clear the tears that blurred my vision. The ad was clear and to the point. "Please help me find my baby girl's lost dog," it said. "$1,000 Reward."

"Thank you anyway," I said in a wobbly voice. "Do you mind if I keep this newspaper?"

Mom and Dad visited me that night. "Daddy," I said, "you and I have some things to talk about."

That's when Mom spilled the beans: "He's been looking everywhere for Muffin. He gets in the car and drives all over, calling out the window. And he's been telling people to call and to pray for you."

I couldn't believe my ears. Now I had to ask him about the biggest surprise of all. "Daddy," I said, "what about the reward money?"

He shuffled his feet. "Well," he said, "I figured it was the only way that dog could be found."

"But a thousand dollars? Daddy, that's so much money! You've never splurged like that. What about always saving for a rainy day?"

Daddy fixed his eyes on a crack in his brown leather shoe. "Sweetheart," he said, "the day you lost your little Muffin I felt the biggest downpour of my life. You were so sad, I would have given anything to get your dog back for you. I'm sorry she hasn't come home."

I thought of all the scrimping and saving Dad must have done to put away a thousand dollars and how quick he was now to give it up for me. The years suddenly faded, and I was once more the girl who had learned bargaining from the best horse trader in the business. You can't put a dollar figure on love, but Dad had come up with "a rare one" of his own. Nothing was too much for my happiness.

"Thank you, Dad," I said, my voice breaking.

This story has a bittersweet ending. Muffin never turned up, but my prayers that she was okay did a lot to comfort me. Eventually, Dad took me back to the pound, and I brought home one of those howling mutts that was yearning for a home. It wasn't a replacement for my lost dog—nothing could take the place of Muffin—but this was a new dog to spoil to my heart's content. I named her Cleo, and we had many happy years together. And from that point on, Dad and I had an understanding. He can complain all he wants about the money I spend, and I can spoil my dog as much as I want.

Love can express itself in many different ways. I realize that when I was young, Daddy worked hard to be a good provider, saving for a rainy day. Then, as now, he was sheltering his baby girl, and giving me love the best way he knew how.

The Return of Roscoe

Shari Smyth

Light from an almost-full moon shone through the window on Roscoe, my old black Lab. He lay dozing by the fire, his graying muzzle twitching, his arthritic legs pawing the air in the long-forgotten rhythm of running. In his sleep he yipped, puppylike.

"Hey, Roscoe, old boy," I said. Where were his dreams taking him? Was he tearing off again across a field and into the woods, hot on the scent of a squirrel? Or was he remembering that first year when I had such big plans for him? The wind howled down the chimney, scattering sparks from the fire. Roscoe woke with a jolt. Stiffly he got up and hobbled over, resting his head on my lap. He'd never been a cuddler, but he liked having his ears scratched. In human years Roscoe was ninety-one. I was fifty-seven. We had come a long way together. I ran a hand along his bumpy bones. A contented sigh seeped from him. Really, is there anything sweeter than an old dog?

I lifted a velvety ear and touched the tattoo that marked him with the noble purpose for which he'd been bred. That was thirteen years ago, but it seemed only yesterday that I carried him, a wiggling eight-week-old bundle, into my house.

With my four teenagers scattering to do their own thing, my work as a mom was winding down. Raising this little guy would keep me busy. At least he needed me to look after him. Inside the door, I pulled out a chair, sat the pup on my knee and gave him a little speech. "Somewhere out there is a blind person whose life you will change," I said. "My job is to love you, build your confidence, and teach you manners so you'll be ready for your trainer." Roscoe licked my face.

He had been born at the Guiding Eyes for the Blind breeding farm in Patterson, New York, not far from where we lived. I would have him for a year. Then he'd go back and be tested for the rigorous schooling it took to be a blind person's eyes. Roscoe's bloodlines were awesome, the folks at Guiding Eyes told me. They'd pointed out his parents' portraits, prominently, even reverently, displayed in their office.

"You've got a lot to live up to, Roscoe," I said, then couldn't help laughing as he bounded out of my lap and went after his rubber bone. "I'm going to raise you right so that all your good qualities come out."

Too quickly he grew from a sweet lap-sitter to a big-boned, handsome dog with a face full of expression. He had boundless energy. Even the kids couldn't keep up. Roscoe never got tired of playing fetch, his outsized paws pounding the turf. He was a graceful swimmer, steering with his tail after a ball in the lake. His bark was a deep woof, woof, woof.

"He's some macho dog," the FedEx man said, backing away as Roscoe, looking like a canine Arnold Schwarzenegger, accompanied me to the door. But his tail went *thump, thump, thump.*

Because he was a future guide dog, Roscoe went everywhere with me. The library, the supermarket, restaurants, church. He wore a blue Guiding Eyes jacket that fit well around his muscular black frame. Wherever we went people oohed and ahhed. The local paper even did a spread on him. "We'll be at this big guy's graduation," the editor promised.

What a proud day that would be! I pictured Roscoe leading his new owner across the stage to get their joint diploma. Sure, I'd miss him terribly. But knowing I'd helped him live up to his famous parents' bloodline would be well worth it.

In the meantime, I collected memories: The sly way Roscoe dropped his empty dish at our feet, or averted his guilty eyes when he'd done something bad. The way he pranced with joy at the sight of his leash. And how he gave forth a long dramatic sigh when he settled down each night, as if the weight of the world were on his shoulders.

One summer Sunday Roscoe was lying in the aisle at church, paws crossed, when Father Mark's sermon went into overtime. The congregation shifted in the pews restlessly. Sensing the general discontent, Roscoe tilted his face heavenward and howled. "Okay, I'm almost finished, Roscoe," Father Mark said to appreciative laughter.

Later, at the communion rail, Roscoe put his head down, repentant. Father Mark reached across and laid an affectionate hand on him. "Bless this dog, Lord, and prepare him for the future you have called him to."

The day before we were to return Roscoe to Guiding Eyes, I took him for a long walk around the lake. A sudden wind came up, churning the water with whitecaps, and there was a distant crack as though a branch had fallen. Roscoe lifted his head, his nostrils quivering. In the blink of an eye he was off, ripping the leash from my hand.

What on earth had gotten into him?

I found him miles away on the other side of the lake, wet and muddy, his long retriever nose plowing the ground. "Roscoe, you're never going to be a guide dog if you behave like this," I said. He looked up at me, the mischievous gleam in his amber eyes not all that different from my son Jon's when he skipped out on homework to go skateboarding with his friends. "All right, big guy, let's go home."

The next day I packed his things in a paper bag: rubber bone, teeth-marked dish, stuffed toy, blue jacket. We drove to Guiding Eyes, Roscoe sprawled comfortably across the back seat.

The woman at the desk greeted us. "Oh, yes, we know Roscoe," she said. "He's going to make a wonderful guide dog." Roscoe wagged his tail and looked up at me. He kept on wagging as they led him away. I gathered his old leash and took it to the empty car. I cried all the way home.

Two weeks later I got a phone call from Guiding Eyes. "Shari, we're going to have to release Roscoe. He's just not cut out for the program."

"What do you mean?" It was just as shocking as if one of my children had been expelled.

"He's a wonderful dog, but he's just too impulsive at times. Skittish too." Apparently, during a training exercise, he'd panicked at a car backfiring.

"Was it me? What did I do wrong?" I'd been clear and direct in my commands. I'd disciplined him carefully. I'd been there for him.

"You didn't do anything wrong, Shari. Dogs aren't machines. They have their own personalities."

So my Guiding Eyes dropout came home. It was as if he'd never left. He went right to his spot in the back of the car when I drove carpool. At the kids' games I'd cheer and Roscoe would join in with his baritone woof, woof, woof, though I suspected he'd rather be chasing down the softball himself. He was part of our family, no question. Still, I wondered if I had failed him. Wasn't he meant for something more meaningful than warming the foot of our bed?

The kids graduated and left home. Instead of settling into a comfortable, carefree retirement (from being a full-time mom, at least), I went through all kinds of ups and downs: One daughter's struggle with, and eventual recovery from, drug and alcohol addiction. Another's insistence on living far from home. A son's leaving his job to indulge his wanderlust. An unexpected move from New York, where we'd spent almost two decades, to Tennessee. A wrenching yearlong separation from my husband that ended in the joyful renewal of our marriage vows.

Now, sitting by the fire, I looked at my old friend Roscoe, sticking by me as he had through all those uncertain times. He kept me company on long strolls through the unfamiliar Tennessee woods. He punctuated my solitary days writing at the computer with the thump, thump, thump of his tail on the rug at my feet. He laid his head in my lap just when I felt most lonely and unloved.

"You weren't meant to be a guide dog," I said. "God meant you for something else." I scratched Roscoe's ears. "He meant you for me."

The Dog
Next Door

Grace Chamberlain

Why won't that yappy little thing shut up?" I muttered that warm April evening, pulling aside the curtain and peering out into the yard we shared with the elderly woman who lived in the other half of our rental duplex. Her scruffy black poodle mix, Sheeba, was at it again, pacing along the fence, barking ferociously at passing cars. Who knew such a small animal could make such a huge racket? The mail carrier, the UPS man, and I had all had our run-ins with her. Or I should say, we'd all had to run from her snapping jaws. It didn't take long for everyone to figure out: Stay away from Sheeba!

I hadn't had much trouble doing that lately, considering I could barely muster the energy to get out of the house. I let the curtain drop and sank back onto the couch. At least my neighbor would take the dog inside for the night, so I'd have quiet till morning. If only there could be a reprieve from the darkness that haunted me, a way out of the funnel of despair that threatened to suck me in ever deeper.

Depression had shadowed my life as far back as I could remember, long before I learned the clinical name for how I felt. I was the last of three girls in a home riven by our father's drinking, and from a very young age, I knew our family was different from the others in our working-class neighborhood. I sensed that I too was different. Other kids seemed so light-hearted and carefree. Most of the time I was sad, lonely, and afraid. My parents were so consumed by their fighting it often seemed as if they forgot I was even there. They would erupt at each other, then lapse into a loaded silence that left me cringing in expectation of the next explosion.

I constantly looked for escapes back then, ways I could, however briefly, grab hold of happiness. Once my father asked me to get him a beer. I couldn't resist taking just a sip. Then another. A giddiness bubbled through me, a glow that seemed to come from inside, pushing aside the sadness. *How come Mother says drinking is bad when it makes you feel so good?* I wondered.

It was kind of like the feeling I got tagging along to Sunday school with the kids down the street. My family did not attend church, so the Bible stories the teacher read were new to me. I couldn't hear enough about God miraculously lifting the burdens of the lowliest people. *Maybe someday, God,* I'd pray, *you'll even come to help me.*

My favorite haven was right next door, with Mr. and Mrs. Matheson, an older couple whose own child was grown. I don't recall what drew me over there initially, but I know what made me keep coming back. It was what I sensed overflowing in their house like tension did in mine, what I savored in Mrs. Matheson's hearty cooking, what I saw sparkling in Mr. Matheson's eyes when he opened the door and found me standing there: love.

Mrs. Matheson and I tackled the dishes as a team; she washed, I dried. Mr. Matheson and I picked pears in the backyard and admired the birds that flocked to the four-story hotel (it was too grand to be a simple birdhouse) he built for them.

Then when I was seven, Mr. Matheson died, and Mrs. Matheson moved away. Not long after that, my parents' marriage broke up. I slipped into despair, as if the ground I'd just been finding my footing on crumbled beneath me. "I feel like I'm falling into a big black hole," I cried to God, "and there's no one to catch me." My mother tried her best, but her hollow expression told me there was only so much she was able to give.

At sixteen, I quit school, left home, and got married, thinking that would make things better. But my husband and I were both so young, we weren't ready to truly share our lives with each other. Again I fell into that despair, an abyss not even God—or the three wonderful children he blessed me with—could save me from.

I got divorced at thirty-one and worked a number of jobs, struggling to raise the kids on my own. How I wished I could embrace life as they did—freely and joyfully. I turned to an escape I remembered from my childhood: alcohol. That first experience with the forbidden beer hadn't been a fluke. Drinking brought me out of the darkness like nothing else could.

But was I doomed to repeat family history? The weary, defeated woman I saw in the mirror reminded me of my mother. And like my father, I drank. If I hadn't had my kids to look after, I would have just stayed in bed and drowned my sorrows. Eventually, though, alcohol stopped doing what it used to. The highs became more and more fleeting, the lows more desolate and unendurable.

I was forty and my kids almost grown before I got help. A faint memory of those Bible stories I'd clung to as a child sent me to a church near where we lived, more out of desperation than hope. In early December 1980, there was an altar call. "Come forward and open your life to God," the pastor urged. "Ask him to take away your problems and fears and replace them with faith."

That was what I wanted, more than anything! Slowly, I made my way to the altar. "God, I need you in my life," I pleaded. "I can't go on like this."

Not two weeks later, I was watching a Sunday-morning church program on TV. The guest was a priest named Father Martin who talked about his out-of-control drinking. "I didn't care about anything but my next drink," he said. "I had a sickness, a disease. It was only through the Twelve Steps of Alcoholics Anonymous that I was healed."

I went to my first AA meeting in January 1981 and quit drinking. But where was that peace Father Martin had promised? "I thought things were supposed to get better once I got sober," I complained to a friend from AA.

"Grace, living sober goes a lot deeper than just not drinking," she said. "You have to learn to deal with all the feelings your drinking used to cover up." She suggested I seek counseling.

In therapy, I discovered that the loneliness, fear, and despondency that had long defined my life weren't signs of some personal weakness. They were symptoms of depression, a disease that for me proved far more intractable than alcoholism. I lost track of all the counselors and psychiatrists and medications I tried over the years. Nothing worked. The darkness might recede for a little while, but it was always there, looming, threatening to swallow me completely. One doctor admitted, "I don't know that we can expect more improvement. I'm afraid your depression is chronic, Grace."

So that's it, I thought numbly. *Nothing will ever change.*

In my late forties, my depression became so overwhelming I was forced to go on disability. How could I work when most days it took everything I had just to get out of bed? It was a good thing my husband—I had remarried in 1987—could support us. My kids were concerned that I couldn't summon the energy to play with my grandchildren. *God, you healed my alcoholism. Can't you help with my depression too?*

I clung to that hope even as I became a prisoner of my illness, reduced to watching from my living-room couch as the world passed me by. That warm April evening I dragged myself off to bed thinking, *You've sunk to a new low if the biggest excitement in your life comes from the yappy little dog next door.*

The same high-pitched barks woke me in the morning. That was odd. My neighbor never left her dog out overnight. My husband and our landlady went to check on her. She had died during the night of heart failure.

Our landlady asked us to help find the dog a home. But who wanted a bad-tempered biter like Sheeba? My husband let her into our side of the duplex. "We can't leave her all alone," he said. "You can drop her off at the pound tomorrow."

I watched the poodle skitter around our living room, her fur so filthy and matted you couldn't see her eyes. "No chance someone will adopt her looking like that," I said. "And I don't want to be stuck with her. I'll have to take her to a groomer." Under my breath, I prayed, "Lord, please find this dog a home."

The earliest appointment I could get with a groomer was in two days. At bedtime I used a baby gate to pen the dog in the kitchen. "You haven't barked or nipped at me once so far," I said. "There might be hope for you yet. Maybe someone will want you if you have a cuter name, like . . . Petunia." I couldn't be sure, but I thought her tail wagged at that.

I was about to drift off to sleep when I heard her whimpering in the kitchen. What could I do but open the gate? I went back up to the bedroom, Petunia right on my heels. Reluctantly, I draped a towel at the foot of the bed. She jumped on it, curled up and fell sound asleep. I stayed awake for a while, just watching her sleep, glad she was so content.

The next day Petunia trailed me all over the house. "I know you don't want a dog," my husband remarked, "but that dog sure wants you."

I shook my head. I just wasn't up to looking after a high-strung dog. I could barely take care of myself.

"I'll try my best," the groomer said doubtfully the day I brought Petunia in. "But I don't know . . . "

I went back later to pick Petunia up. I looked around the shop but didn't see her. "Where's the dog?" I asked.

"She's right behind you."

I turned. There stood a black ball of fluff with a tiny pink bow on her collar. "Petunia?" At the sound of my voice, her tail wagged so fast it blurred. She peered up at me, her shoe-button eyes shining, telling me something I'd never expected. *I trust you,* those bright black eyes seemed to say. *I need you. I love you.*

In that instant, my resistance melted. Petunia belonged with me.

I took her to the vet for a checkup. He found several bad teeth. "I'll take those out. They're probably the cause of her biting," he said. "But as far as her disposition, don't expect much improvement. It's most likely the result of some early trauma. An older dog just isn't capable of changing that much."

I stood there, dumbfounded. Where had I heard that before? I was thinking about myself, of course, thinking about how I'd become resigned to believing nothing would change, that I would go on with my heart sealed off to life, a chronic depressive fumbling through the darkness and only occasionally stumbling upon a bit of happiness—the love of a neighbor or the laugh of a grandchild; even the sight of a small, unkempt dog sleeping peacefully at the foot of my bed.

It seemed so odd to me that a lifelong struggle against such a stubborn foe would come down to this one moment in a vet's office. I turned to Petunia, who was quietly looking up at me from the examining table, her gaze warm and trusting. She'd changed so much already! Was God showing me that I would change too if I opened myself completely to his love? That those seemingly fleeting moments of happiness could take over my life like despair had, if I would only trust the power of his love in a way I had never dared?

We left the vet's office together, my dog and I, and headed home. "You're a beautiful, precious girl," I told Petunia, amazed at what a difference love can make.

Gypsy

Claire Warren

We're quite similar, Gypsy and I, and that's partly why I came by her. Christmas 1984. . . . Grimmy was brown and curly, half poodle, half curly retriever; the father, a grey schnauzer. I visited them—six fluffy balls. The others tumble-ran to the front of the box. *Pick me! Pick me!* Gypsy hung back, just watching. My heart went out to her. *That's the one: the little shy one; the tiny ball of black wool with big brown eyes and the cutest nose shining from within a windmill of fur.*

When we brought her home, she didn't cry, just sat quietly, looking and learning. She was always with me: she became my shadow—sometimes in front, but never far away. At night when I would call her, thinking she had wandered off, she was there at my feet; a soft touch on my leg with her nose to announce her presence—my shadow even in darkness.

She has put a lot of joy into the world in sixteen-and-a-half years, caused a lot of smiles and softness. She has a particular way with little old ladies. So many of them have had a small dog just like her, who lived to a ripe old age. "I love scruffy little dogs," perfect strangers would say, and she would beam back up at them. A friendly little bunyip, and multi-faceted: serving as hot-water bottle, clothes and seat warmer, rug realigner, cushion scatterer, doorbell alert, chief cat bowl washer-upper, burglar disperser, tour guide—she even played guitar at Bridget's wedding. She's been acknowledged in books; had her photo in the *Age*, seated among nuns; and been mistaken for both a handbag and a cushion.

We were so in tune that she always knew when I would be home. About ten minutes before I arrived, she would go to the front door, or climb onto the back of the sofa to look out the window, on full alert. . . . When I started working from home she was overjoyed, but also aware of the need for balance in life. So if the day had been too single-mindedly work-oriented, she would remind me with a touch on my leg so gentle that, if I were totally focused, it would not disturb me but, if I were at all open to a walk, I would look down into those expressive, soft, brown eyes, and a deal would be struck.

Without her, I never would have walked in half the places we explored: back lanes; parks at dusk; quiet, brooding places. She let me know if they were safe or not, whether people approaching were goodies or baddies—she was quick to pick up vibes.

She was an undemanding dog. On our walks she was happy to do her own thing while I solved the problems of the world in my head. She didn't need to be chasing sticks or balls and, if she did, she seldom brought them back. Why should she? But she did like me to throw pine cones, which presented a challenge with their unpredictable bounce. She often claimed one as a souvenir, and would keep it for those idle moments when she was guarding the car. Of course, pine cones have seeds which fall out when chewed, and old Volkswagens often leak. A miniature pine forest along the back window ledge of my blue VW reached five centimeters before dying in the summer drought.

She was perceptive and learned quickly, sometimes from a mistake: baths are hot, and weight is better in the car than out the window. Prickles in foot: stand still and hold up to show me which one. Flea-hunting: roll over to show me where to look. I spoke to her as if she should understand every word, so her vocabulary was huge. Sometimes she wrestled with the concepts, but she pronounced the words "Good Morning" and "Hello" with exactly my intonation.

And she worked out some things that truly amazed me. One night we were sleeping in a loft reached by a vertical ladder. I carried her up, holding on with one hand, but she herself solved the problem of how to come down. I climbed down a few rungs so my shoulders were level with the loft floor. She put her front feet on my shoulders and I scooped her up with my free arm.

She had never run with horses, but knew to stay clear of their hooves and show respect. On a day ride, when I'd been in the saddle for hours, she sussed out how to get a pat. She ran ahead to some high ground; then, as we came by on the track, there she was waiting, at arm-height. Once she followed me about fifteen feet up a huge laurel tree—oh sure, it was an easy climb, like a staircase, but she did it. And when I took her to meet an elephant at a circus, I think she thought she was in the shadow of a tall building. When she realized this was an animal, she freaked totally and dived between my legs. Mind you, this was after the lion had unexpectedly roared at us.

She could count to at least ten. I played cricket in summer and, on one stinking, scorching day far too hot for a sensible black dog to run out to the wicket to join the celebrations, she slept in the cool pavilion. Only when the last wicket fell did she come flying out on to the pitch. That boggled a few minds.

There were just a few points on which we differed. She never liked the way I kept rugs straight; she preferred instead to scruff them up to provide a couple of layers of softness between her poodleness and the floorboards. She decided early that she'd like to be a bit scruffy. Even so, she loved being brushed—particularly if it interrupted my cat being brushed—though she was really precious of her moustache and beard, so forget-me-not seeding was a horror time of year.

I adore that little dog and, in all those years, we spent only fourteen days apart. Because she went everywhere with me, she became remarkably socialized. At book launches and exhibition openings, I tracked her progress around the crowd, listening to her recognize the legs she knew. I love the way she greets her friends—such boundless, unbridled enthusiasm. Her especially favourite people cause her to scream with delight. I love the way she insists people acknowledge her with eye contact and a hello. A pat makes her happy.

She's amazed me often and taught me a lot, and from me she's learned the etiquette of dinner parties, exhibitions, cricket matches; and how to behave on trams and in shops.

She had a wicked sense of humour, thinking it funny to bark in the library-quiet of the bank and watch everyone jump. In pet shops she loved window-shopping—sniffing along rows of dog food and treats. Once she shoplifted some rabbit pellets.

One day we were walking in Studley Park in Melbourne—a huge park, wild in spots, tracing the Yarra River around the bottom of the Kew hills. Gypsy rolling in lush grass. I walk on, expecting her to gallop past me. After a while, I turn. No little black curly person in sight. Walk back to where I'd last seen her, rolling on the bank. Nothing. She's gone back to the car. Climbing to the top of the hill and calling. No sign of her. Calling. Calling. Desperation. Thought I heard a noise—like when she's asking to come in the back door. Another call and she responds. Down the hill, running. "Gypsy!" A moaned "He-e-elp." Keep calling to get location. Mostly she responds. I'm quite close now. I'm nearly back where I last saw her. Where is she? Calling, calling. Nothing. Call again. Here! She answers. I've passed her. Go back. Call. From below me, she answers. I lean over the bank to look. There she is perched on a snag in the river like a mountain goat, all four feet bunched together. She had been so into her rolling that she rolled right off the bank into the river, and couldn't climb back up.

She loved surprises: that little face lit up at the first smell of ozone or the eucalyptus heralding her farm birthplace. But best of all was our ritual after-dinner hunt for the hidden dog treats. There were only ever three, but she would always look hopefully for more—and once or twice there were.

On her last day she did something truly amazing. She could hardly walk, and the need to go outside for a wee came on quicker than she could manage. But this time she waited at the front door for me to open it, stumbled to the front gate and waited, then walked to the grass for the wee. Then, she walked to the end of our fence and sniffed where it joined our neighbour's. She turned and walked back past the gate to where our other neighbour's fence joined ours and checked that out. Once inside again, she went out the back. We carried her down the steps and she looked up the side of the house, then walked to the near corner, under the lemon tree. She paused at that spot and came back the long way, past the veggie garden and in behind the fish pond to check out the hidden corner. I think she was making a map of our home, so that her soul can watch over us from heaven.

My eighteen-year-old cat Polly has kept a vigil beside the grave since Gypsy landed there. It may be that that's the best spot for catching the winter sun, but perhaps their bond was greater than even I knew. Anyway, I know where I'll bury Polly.

Gypsy had a wonderful sense of humour. Exactly a week after she died, she sent me a white cat. I know it was her, because he has one blue and one yellow eye, the colours of the *Dianella tasmanica* (flax lily) flowers which I planted beside her. This Mr. Alby Fluffybum has lifted me out of my sadness and made me laugh—a good present. Perhaps when he is two years old, as Polly was when we brought Gypsy down from the farm, I will be ready for another little dog.

I can see Gypsy's place from the window—a mound of

brightly coloured gum leaves, petals and flowers, brought home for her, to let her know where I've been—today, a spray of wattle and a cockatoo feather from Studley Park. For when we'd been out together, she'd always brought home a collection of assorted flora stuck to her hairy little legs.

The oaks are whispering; the wind plays tricks on me. It causes the bead curtain at the back door to click and I look up expecting to see Gypsy come out on to the verandah, checking what I'm up to. I miss playing hide-and-seek with her in the park, and driving on winter nights when she would climb onto my lap and lean her whole body back against mine, head on my shoulder, sharing body warmth.

I miss my little black shadow and the soft nudge of her nose on my leg saying, "I'm here." Ancient Egyptians believed that whenever you say a person's name, they are still alive. "Gypsy. Gypsy. Gypsy."

Remember
This Promise

Roberta Messner

D riving down East Pea Ridge Road on a chilly evening last February, I squinted into the darkness, trying to ignore the throbbing pain behind my left eye. I was on my way home from an all-day conference that had been billed as a booster shot for flagging faith. I'd needed it in the worst possible way. Chronic illness had affected every area of my life. My work as a nurse once brought great joy; now just getting through my shift was a daily battle. Doctors' bills ate up my savings. Too often I canceled meetings with friends when pain struck. Folks eventually stopped making plans with me.

The worst part was the emptiness I felt, as if illness had blotted out my true self. I couldn't sense God anymore. Even getting down on my knees and praying out loud didn't seem to help. I tried writing out my prayers in a journal. But my confused ramblings looked so ugly in contrast to the pretty rose-sprigged pages that I tore out all my entries and ripped them to pieces.

The conference had been my last hope, but a latecomer had squeezed into my row, hefting a backpack loaded with books. The backpack hit me square in the eye, giving me a blinding headache. I rushed from the building to my car, eager to get home to an ice bag and my bed.

I was headed down East Pea Ridge Road when I heard a sickening thump, followed immediately by a yelp of pain. My foot slammed down on the brake pedal. I looked frantically over my shoulder and saw a mass of fur on the road. "Oh, no!" I cried. I'd hit a dog!

I jumped out of the car and hurried through a group of onlookers. I dropped to my knees on the road next to the dog and stroked her soft fur. She was badly hurt, bleeding profusely and barely moving. "Jesus. Oh, Jesus," was all I could say. But I knew God wasn't listening. How could something like this have happened if he were?

A young man crouched beside me. "I'm a vet's assistant," he said. "Looks like she's got a broken hip. Maybe some internal injuries. You could take her to the animal ER, but they'll probably end up putting her to sleep." He looked the dog over while rubbing her ear. "No collar. Most likely a stray."

"She can't die!" I said helplessly. Just as the words left my lips, an inner voice took command: *Trust me, Roberta. Let me take care of everything.*

"If you want," the man said, "I'll take her to the ER in my car. You can follow."

I ran to my trunk and took out a thick antique rug I'd bought recently. The man and I lifted the dog onto it. By the time we got her loaded into the back of his car, the rug was soaked through with blood.

I followed close behind during the twenty-mile trip to

the animal ER. My head still pounded, but that didn't seem important anymore. Nothing mattered except saving that injured dog. Yet doubts crowded out my prayers. What does God care about a dog? What does God care about you? You're just one person in a world teeming with people in need. Again the inner voice spoke: *Let me.*

I flew into the parking lot and pulled up next to the man's car. I dashed inside, got to the check-in desk and blurted, "I'm the woman who hit the dog that young man just brought in. Do they think they can save her?" The receptionist avoided my eyes. "Number where you can be reached?" she asked.

I gave her the information, then collapsed into a chair in the corner. Finally someone called my name. I followed a woman to a room with a metal table. On it was the dog, bandaged all over with an IV in one of her front legs. Despite her injuries and the harsh fluorescent light, she looked beautiful— a grayish brown German shepherd mix. I imagined she was a watchdog for some family. I leaned over and gently kissed the top of her head. "I'm so sorry I hurt you," I whispered. "I didn't mean to. You know that, don't you?" Her eyes remained closed.

It was just one thing after another—my illness; getting smacked by the backpack; hitting this dog. I wished I could help her but I couldn't even help myself.

Desperate, I cupped the dog's face in my hands and began talking out loud, forgetting about the vet and assistants in the room. "I don't know how to help you," I told the dog. "But I know someone who does. God knows everything about you. He made you. He wants the best for you." My words startled me. They were promises I'd once clung to, my belief in them instilled and nurtured by years of Sunday school, church, Bible reading and prayer. But my faith had been beaten down by illness. A picture formed in my mind. It was Jesus, gazing down at the dog with eyes of such compassion that they took in every cell, every molecule, of her body.

"I have to go home now," I told the dog at last. "But don't worry. God will be with you. He's watching over you as if you're the only dog in the whole world."

"Promise me one thing," I said to the vet. "Don't put her to sleep without calling me." Then I thanked the young man who'd brought the dog in, and left.

When I got home I put an ice bag on my head and fell into bed. I tried to sleep, but two images kept appearing in my mind: the dog bleeding on the road and Jesus gazing down at her in the animal hospital. *Why did you let me hit that dog? Why weren't you watching over me too, Lord? I feel so lost.*

In the darkness and silence of my bedroom, the inner voice answered. *You are never lost, Roberta. Every day, every instant, I watch over you as if you were the only one in the world. I am with you, even in your suffering.*

There in the stillness of the night, that voice seemed to reverberate through my very being. I felt myself relax. My pain subsided—not just the pain in my head, but also the pain deep inside me. I drifted off to sleep. The ringing phone woke me in the morning. I picked up the receiver hesitantly. "This is a fine dog you've got here," a male voice said. "You can come pick her up anytime." Pick her up? There must have been some mistake. *Please don't let them have put her to sleep,* I prayed, then got dressed.

At the ER the dog raised her head and greeted me with a bark. She was still bandaged, but the IV was gone.

Again I cupped her face in my hands. "Are you really all right?" She barked once more, a happy, healthy bark that said, "Let's get out of here!" The vet couldn't explain her recovery. "She's one lucky dog," was all he could say.

I took her home and put an ad in the paper. The next morning a man called me. "That dog sounds like our Lucy. She lifted the latch on the storm door and got out the other day. Looks like she wiggled out of her collar too; it's still here on the living-room floor. I tell you, we've been worried sick."

We agreed to meet each other later that day. The man was sitting on a concrete bench when I arrived. The dog jumped up and licked his face, her tail a blur. It was his Lucy all right.

Introducing myself, I explained to him about the accident. "I am so sorry. I feel just terrible," I said.

"I'm just relieved she's not lost," he said, rubbing her ears. "The kids haven't stopped crying since she ran off."

He tried to pay me for the vet bill, but I was having none of it. After all, I was feeling restored myself, at least spiritually. And isn't that where true healing always takes place—in the soul rather than the body?

I watched them pull out of the parking lot. Lucy clambered over the backseat and pressed her nose to the rear window. I could swear she was looking right at me. We were both going home.

Sometimes Angels Have Tails

Carolyn Anne Anderson

I grew up in Balsam Lake, Wisconsin, a very small Midwestern town where my father was pastor of the Lutheran church. Nearly every week, in Sunday school and during my dad's sermons, I heard about angels. I believed in them, but I didn't think I'd ever actually see one. After all, they were flying around "out there" serving God, far-removed from the nitty-gritty details of the world. They had more important things to worry about than what happened in my day-to-day life. And until I was seventeen years old, that life was pretty ordinary.

Then, one summer day in 1991, I was in a terrible car accident. In the hospital, I was told my spinal cord had been severed, and that as a result I was paralyzed from the waist down and would be confined to a wheelchair for the rest of my life. I didn't really believe the prognosis until the doctor held up the results of my MRI and pointed out where the damage had taken place. As soon as I saw it, I cried. *What happens now, God?* I wondered.

I was in intensive care for a few weeks, and in a full-body cast for about three months. Thanks to the support of my family and friends, I was able to work on my recovery. "Everyone is praying for you, Carolyn," my parents told me. Indeed it seemed all of Balsam Lake pulled together, holding all sorts of benefits to raise money to help pay my medical bills. It moved me that people cared so much. Yet the thought of being paralyzed for the rest of my life was still too much for me to comprehend fully.

After I got out of the hospital, I returned home and went on to finish my senior year of high school. When it was time to choose a college, I decided on the University of Arizona in Tucson. There I wouldn't have to deal with the difficulties of trying to maneuver a wheelchair in the snow and cold. Aside from the weather, the landscape and architecture were also more wheelchair-friendly. I'd have to move far from my family and friends, but I thought the change would do me good, and I wanted to prove to myself that I could make it on my own.

I loved it at first. The climate was perfect. I had a specially adapted car that enabled me to drive, and I loved cruising through the desert under the blazing sun. But I found it hard to make friends in this new city. The university alone had more people than my entire hometown. Have I made a terrible mistake?

I threw myself into my classes, but my loneliness only grew. For the first time, really, I began to think about what the accident had done to me. I'm stuck in this wheelchair for the rest of my life. *Don't you even care, God?* I complained in my prayers. But I never got any answer. Eventually I decided God was concerned with more important things than me and my problems. I stopped praying altogether, and grew increasingly bitter and angry about how my life had been derailed.

People always treated me differently when they saw my wheelchair, but now it began to grate on my nerves. Almost daily someone asked, "Do you need some help?" More often than not I snapped back, "No! I don't need any help!" Some talked so loudly when they spoke to me that they were practically yelling. "My hearing is fine," I'd snarl. Children in the supermarket pointed and stared. So did their parents, sometimes. Other times folks treated me as if I were a child, and occasionally even patted me on the head. *If people can't understand and accept me for who I am,* I started to think, *then why bother having anything to do with them?*

I started spending all day in bed feeling sorry for myself. If I bothered to get up at all, most of the time I didn't even leave the house. One night it got to be too much for me, and I broke down crying. "Dear God," I said, "I can't take this anymore. I need a companion, someone who understands me." I felt guilty, because it had been so long since I'd talked to God instead of just complaining, but the words kept coming. "I want a relationship in which this wheelchair will never be an issue. I need someone who'll be there for me all the time, day in and day out."

I was praying to find a man, but it seemed God was in no hurry to send one my way. So in 1996 when I heard about Handi-dogs—a local organization that trains dogs to help people with disabilities—I figured man's best friend was the next-best thing. I called them up and was told, "We just got a black Labrador retriever puppy. Why don't you come see him?" That's how I met Tyler. He was the most adorable dog I'd ever seen, and I fell in love with him as soon as I looked into his dark-brown eyes. I took him home after arranging a schedule for our training sessions, which would start a month later.

I'd never had a dog, though, and didn't realize what I was getting myself into. Like any puppy, Tyler chewed things. I'd come home to a carpet strewn with the remains of books or shoes. Once, I found my white futon cover smeared with blue ink. There were chewed-up bits of a ballpoint pen scattered around. "Tyler!" I demanded. "Did you do that?" He looked up at me with what seemed to be a smile, and I saw his teeth were blue.

When he wasn't destroying my possessions, he was leaving other sorts of messes in the backyard. Or eating. It seemed I was always at the store buying dog food. He'd gobble it down just as fast as I filled his bowl. He was growing rapidly, and was harder than ever to control. I was relieved when it was finally time to start his training sessions.

I met a lot of people there—trainers as well as other disabled folks. For the first time since I'd moved to Tucson, I started to feel like I was part of a community. And as I went back each week, I opened up and made friends. "It's so hard with Tyler sometimes," I confided to one woman. "If he doesn't get enough exercise, he gets hyperactive. But sometimes I'm not up to walking him. Besides, he's so strong that he can pull me right out of my wheelchair."

"If you're not up to walking Tyler yourself," she told me, "ask someone to walk him for you."

Ask someone? "I can't do that," I protested.

"Tyler's here to be of service to you. If you can accept that from a dog, why can't you accept it from a person?"

I had to admit she was right. Still, it was humbling the first time I asked my next-door neighbor, Carl, if he would take Tyler for a walk, but he gladly did it. "Ya ever need me again," he said when they returned from a jog around the neighborhood, "just give a holler." Then there was the time I asked someone in the supermarket if he could carry the forty-pound bag of dog food out to my car for me. He looked at the bag then at Tyler, smiled and said, "No problem." Maybe it was then I saw there was something special about this dog, not just for me but for everyone who met him.

As the training progressed, Tyler grew into a calm, gentle, and reliable companion. He learned how to do many things around the house that make life easier for me. He opens and closes doors. He climbs into the dryer, pulls the clothes out and puts them in the laundry basket. He fetches the cordless phone for me. He even helps me make the bed. And when I hold on to his harness, he pulls my wheelchair behind him instead of pulling me out of it.

He does pull me out of my funks, though. Lying in bed all day is no longer an option since Tyler needs to be fed and let out every morning. By the time I've done that, I figure, I'm already out of bed. Might as well stay that way. If it's one of those times when I feel like holing up, Tyler brings me his leash and harness. It's hard to dread the thought of leaving the house when you have a big black dog bouncing with joy every time he hears the jingle of car keys and knows he's going for a ride.

His exuberance is contagious. I see it in the way people relate to me now, and in how I relate to them. I don't get any more awkward silences or overly concerned questions about whether I need help. Instead, people say "I had a Lab who looked just like him" and tell me all about their dog. Children in the store don't point and stare; they run up and ask, "Can I pet him?" And people no longer shout at me as if I were deaf; they baby-talk to Tyler. If that ever makes me feel like saying something snappish, I remind myself that I'd rather have them pat my dog's head than mine. Then I look into Tyler's eyes, he wags his tail, and sweeps that old bitterness away. Just as people have become more accepting of me, I've become more accepting of myself. I've learned that asking for help when I need it is nothing to be ashamed of, and that most people are more than willing to lend a hand.

Tyler has made all the difference in the world. When I think about that, I realize God really does care about the nitty-gritty details of my day-to-day life, and he does answer prayers. I asked him to send me a companion, someone who understood me, who'd be there for me day in and day out, and it wouldn't matter that I was in a wheelchair. I got all that when Tyler came bounding into my life, and more: My neighbor Carl, who helped me out by walking my dog? We were married last March, in a church I joined nearly two years ago. In addition to the traditional best man and groomsmen, we had man's best friend. Tyler was at the church too, and all through the service, he could not stop wagging his tail.

Angels might be "out there" with God, but they're also right here with us. It's just that sometimes they have tails, not wings.

Loyal Friends

and Companions

Lyn and Ralphie

Lyn Zboril

I didn't ever intend to get a dog. I've always liked dogs but have never been crazy about them like some people are. In fact, when people raved on about their dogs, I used to think that they must be lacking in some area of their lives—to be so crazy about their canines, I just couldn't understand it. All that was to change on July 14, 2000.

On that particular day I had arranged to have breakfast with some friends. During the conversation, we discussed dogs and I casually mentioned how, now that I had a backyard, I wouldn't mind getting one—one day. I was nonchalant enough to go to the RSPCA "just for a look." I emphasized that I was not yet ready for the full commitment of dog ownership. When we got there, however, something happened within me. There were so many beautiful animals desperate for attention, desperate for love and a home. As my friend and I walked through a maze of cages, we saw him: a little bundle of dirty white fluff, so scared and frightened that when we put a lead on him for a test walk, he pulled back in fear. The most gorgeous dog I had ever seen. I fell in love.

I named him Ralphie. Ralphie is a Maltese–bichone frisé–terrier cross, and he was a stray, so I know nothing about

90

him. I know now that he has come from a good home because he is very happy and comfortable around people. His age was estimated to be eighteen months. I've had him now for four months, and in that time he has completely transformed my life.

I am forty-one, single, and I have a hectic lifestyle. I have my own hairdressing salon employing four people. I have a wonderful family and have lots of fantastic friends. I had always thought that I was doing okay, but Ralphie brought out something that I hadn't thought existed within me—a love and nurturing so deep that sometimes it frightens me. To receive back such unconditional love is even more scary. He has done for me what no human has ever come close to doing yet—he is bringing down my defences!

I make a point of walking Ralphie around the neighbourhood every morning and night. I'm very glad that I do. One Sunday I took him as usual for his walk, came home, and bathed him. I then had some friends over and we decided to go out for lunch. It was raining so I decided not to take Ralphie and he wasn't very happy about it. (He always manages to break my heart when I leave without him—he looks at me with his big, black eyes and looks so sad!) We all left and returned within two hours. As soon as I walked inside, I knew he was gone. With horror I realized I hadn't put his identification collar back on after his bath! I was distraught. I sobbed uncontrollably and was useless to my friends, who immediately sprang into action. They rang all the dogs' homes, the police, the council, and anyone else that they could think of. They photocopied photographs of him and made posters with

"Reward" written all over them. They went on a neighbour-hood search—in the rain! Meanwhile I was blubbering miserably, totally incapable of doing anything except berating myself for not putting on his collar and taking him with me. I decided that I could at least hang the posters. Still unashamedly weeping, I hung them in supermarkets, laundromats, on streetlights—anywhere I could. A leaflet dropper was looking out for him; a dog walker was doing the same. A friend I met along the way was comforting me while helping me look. I was shattered. My lunchtime companions had done all they could, so they said goodbye. All of this happened within one hour of return from lunch!

I went to the local café for a coffee and to contemplate my life without Ralphie. While sitting there—tears still streaming, coffee going cold, staring into space—my mobile phone rang. It was my neighbour excitedly shouting that he was back home! Home! Ralphie's home? I sprinted back and there he was, happily gnawing his bone, his tail wagging, and totally unaware of the grief he had innocently caused me. When I burst into yet another pool of tears, he walked up to me, looked at me and then gave me a big doggy kiss. He had escaped through a tiny gap between the house and fence and had returned the same way. Ralphie had gone looking for me and found his way back home by "sniffing" his own markings and familiar trail!

This incident, more than any (and there have been a few) drove home to me how much love I have for this little dog. When he was on his walkabout and I was crying in my coffee, images of him played upon my mind. I saw him skip when he was happy, but slink slowly toward me, head down, eyes up, when he was in trouble. I saw him sitting with his face screwed up waiting for the dreaded face washer to clean his mouth and nose after he buried his bones. I saw him trotting around at my gym, jumping onto my stomach and sitting there while I did my abdominal workout. And I realized how much he loved me and how much I loved him.

I wondered how I was going to cope without him—I had never fully realized how deep the bond was that we had formed. I truly believed that all joy would now be gone in my life, and I prayed that he was safe.

It was during that reflection that it hit me. I realized then that all those dog-crazy and loopy people had been right all along. They were not lacking in their lives, but I was. They already knew what had taken me forty-one years to discover, which was that a dog can and will deeply enrich a person's life. The impact of having Ralphie in my life has been overwhelming. He is a dear little thing. He makes me so happy and brings so much joy and fun into my life that I am forever grateful to whatever force was involved in somehow bringing us together—when all I did was to go for breakfast with friends.

Not a Bone to Pick

Ruth Pollack Coughlin

T he first time ever I saw her face, she was six weeks old. Among her seven sisters and brothers, all of whom gained my attention, she was the only one who, when I picked her up, looked me square in the eye and then nestled her tiny head in the hollow of my neck.

I was sold, and she was for sale. It was 1978. It was December, and I had just turned thirty-five. In New York in those days, I had grown tired of taking care of nothing more than a group of plants. Thriving as they were, those plants, they were not showing a lot of heart, and heart was what I needed.

Twenty-five dollars is what the animal shelter on Long Island told me it would take to liberate this creature—silky and black as India ink and a mixture of at least two breeds, with a minuscule diamond of white on her miraculously small breast. On the way home, in the car I had rented to drive across the bridge and bring us back to Gramercy Park, she curled her body next to mine and rested her face on my right thigh.

It is true that she sighed. It is true that I, a woman without children, attempted to understand that this puppy I had just named Lucy was not a child. It is also true that I could feel my own breast swell, my heart fluttering, my mind filled with the possibilities of unconditional love—mine for her, hers for me. Unconditional love. It was something I knew most people felt could only be doled out by a mother, even though many therapists acknowledge that family love, especially mother love, can be as polluted as the biggest and the baddest and the nearest toxic dump.

Lucy, in growing up, ate couches. She ate books and records and pillows and eyeglasses. She nibbled at fine Persian rugs. She ate shoes. She believed that the legs of very good chairs were her personal teething rings; she hid her rawhide bones in the pots of those well-tended plants, and then she would rediscover those bones quite dramatically, fresh dirt strewn across varnished hardwood floors. She scratched, and scratched again, at the surfaces of treasured antique chests.

Rolling against a tide of family and friends who castigated me for accepting such bad-dog behavior, I stood firm. She destroys things, I said. These things are nothing, that's what they are, they're things, they don't live and they don't breathe. She doesn't destroy people. She'll grow out of it, I said. People who destroy people don't ever grow out of it.

And, of course, she grew out of it.

Those who admonished me and never loved Lucy didn't know that for every new couch I bought, that for every pillow or pair of eyeglasses I replaced, I never looked back. They didn't know that Lucy was there during the times about which they knew not.

She was there when I cried, and licked the tears off my

face; she was there when I rejoiced, and cavorted around, laughing with me. She knew what was good and she knew what was bad. When louts were cruel to her, I comforted her; when they were cruel to me, her instinct was such that she curled tighter around me.

Even then, in those early years when the dog-expert books said I should scold her—and I did—she never stopped loving me, nor I her.

No matter what, she would finally smile at me, as only dogs can smile. And always, it would be a smile that went beyond acceptance. It was much more: It was pure. It was without contamination. It was something called love with no baggage, something most therapists would not be able to acknowledge.

She and I, transported both in spirit and in body by the man of our dreams, moved from New York to Michigan when she was five.

He grew to love her, as I knew he would, though at first it was slow going. Here was a man who had trained dogs all his life, and then here was Lucy—untrained except in one thing, loving me. He was the one who finally got it, truly got it, because he knew about a kind of love that held no barriers. Because he knew that this bond between Lucy and me was like our marriage. Incontrovertible.

When Lucy got sick on my birthday last month, exactly thirteen years after the day I first saw her, I was optimistic.

For more than a dozen years, she had never been ill. Requisite shots, yes. Sickness, no. Romping and yapping and wagging her tail in her own inimitable Lucy way, she was perceived by all as a puppy. She was a dog who slept in the sunshine with her front paws crossed; she was a dog who was at my heels wherever I went.

She was someone who finally showed me the meaning of unconditional love. She was a dog who would never die, I thought, a Lucy who would continue to support me, who would be there, a dog who would see me through the darkest of anyone's worst imagination of what the bleakest days would be like.

We went three times, Lucy and I did, during those two weeks in December, to the veterinarian, surely one of the kindest and most compassionate people I have ever known. She was hospitalized, her heart failing, her kidneys not functioning, an IV unit hooked into her beautifully turned right leg, an inelegant patch marking where her once lustrous black fur had been shaved to accommodate the needle.

The vet allowed me to visit, but not for long, and from a distance. It might upset her to see you, he said, and then he added, if she actually does notice you, it might be disruptive for her to watch you leave. Not wanting to add to the pain she was already in, I peered through a window. She was listless, apparently unaware of my presence.

Maybe she couldn't see me, but she could still smell me, the person with whom she had been sleeping for thirteen years, the person who could never tell her enough how much her love was valued. And how I knew, shrinks notwithstanding, that no one could ever get a bead on this, and if they did, they'd probably think it was bonkers and maybe they'd even have to go back to school to figure it out.

This was Lucy who was just barely hanging on, but evidently proud to do even that. My husband and I knew: She was very sick, there would be no recovery. "She doesn't," my husband said to me, "want to leave you."

Lucy and I went back to the vet.

He allowed me some time alone with her, the vet did, after he told me there would be no turnaround. This was a statement made shortly after the one in which he told me that it had to be my decision. Most people, he said, out of a need that is especially self-serving, prolong the lives of their dying dogs.

I knew what I had to do. Her suffering could not go on, not for another day, not for another hour.

For some time, I held her. I thanked her for being such a great pal. I kissed her repeatedly, on the top of her head and on her eyes. On her adorable nose and on her incomparable feet. On every part of the small body I had kissed at least a million times during the past thirteen years. On her setterlike tail, even though she wasn't a setter, a tail that never stopped wagging.

I kissed her on her heart that was failing—a heart that had beaten so well, so true; a heart that could have, in a split second, taught a legion of therapists what unconditional love is really all about.

The other day, I somehow found the guts to open the envelope with the veterinarian's return address. *Euthanasia*, the bill said. *Fifty dollars*.

It seemed to me a small price to pay to allow Lucy, the one who showed me at every turn that she was all heart, to go in peace.

Barney McCabe

Sharon Azar

Barney McCabe, I called him. I found him tied to a storefront on Christmas Day, starving and shivering, abandoned to the streets. I'd seen so many like him before. I had been rescuing dogs for a long time, starting with Baby Bear.

Walking through a city park one afternoon I saw a large Belgian sheep dog tied to a tree. His tongue drooped from his mouth like a tag on a marked-down dress. A cardboard sign read: "Owner died. Please take dog. Very friendly." His long, shaggy locks were well-groomed and he was obviously well fed. Would I take him? Something made me say yes.

I didn't know much about dogs, except they needed to be walked and fed. Taking Baby Bear out in my concrete-and-asphalt neighborhood, I met other dog owners who stopped and gave me advice. Children couldn't help hugging Baby Bear. I made a whole new set of friends.

"Sharon," one of them said to me one day, "I found an abandoned dog down by the river. Can you help me look for a new home for him?"

"Sure," I said. "Whatever I can do." With that I became part of a network of dog rescuers. We posted signs on trees, traded phone calls, and passed information from one to another. It felt like a calling, something God wanted me to do—to give these lonely, often abused animals a new lease on life. Soon I was taking care of dogs for a night or two, until they could be placed, or going on trips to the vet with a foster pet in tow, making sure it was healthy enough for a new home. Some of the dogs stayed.

First came Fonzie, a large male husky someone had left in front of the Metropolitan Museum of Art. One of the curators urged him on me, with a few dollars for his care.

Next came Ginger. I had just lost Baby Bear to old age. Both Fonzie and I were grief-stricken, so when we met a man in the park giving up an eight-month-old Border collie and golden retriever mix, I decided to take her home.

Then came Barney. My friend Norman and I were on our way to a party that Christmas Day several years ago. Bundled up against a bitter wind coming off the Hudson, we made our way through the slushy streets. As we passed the local pet store I saw a black dog roped to the door. The store was closed.

I knelt down with my hands open. The poor creature was trembling uncontrollably, head down against the knifelike wind. His ribs protruded through his dull coat and there were scars on his body. He looked to be part German shepherd and part Labrador.

"It's okay, boy," I said softly. He looked at me, his eyes wary.

"Sharon?" Norman said. I knew what he was concerned about. "You don't have room for another dog, especially a big one like this." He was right, but it was Christmas Day, and I couldn't just walk away.

I let the dog sniff my hand, still talking softly. You could tell he was torn between his fear of people and his instinct for shelter. I cautiously untied the leash, careful not to startle him. "It'll only be for a few days," I told Norman. "Until I can find a home for him." At my apartment I put the stray in the bedroom, away from the other two dogs, left him some food and water and closed the door.

I had no idea what my bedroom would look like when I got home from the party. There was no telling what a scared, abused animal would do, locked in. After greeting Fonzie and Ginger, I edged into the bedroom. The stray was lying on my bed, paws crossed, his eyes searching my face. Nothing was out of place. Even the bowls were right where I had left them, licked clean.

He proved a good houseguest, but a difficult dog to walk. I had to hold him on a short leash. If anyone raised a hand to wave or made a sudden movement, he growled and snarled. He absolutely refused to be touched by anyone but me. "Please, don't pet the dog," I had to say to children. "Not yet. He's not used to people."

I named him Barney McCabe after a farmer's dog I once knew. But that animal had been playful and good-natured. This one was anxious, distrustful. Living in my small apartment became difficult with three dogs—two of them males who fought for their territory. I continued to keep Barney separate from Ginger and Fonzie.

Until then, rescuing dogs had brought me so much comfort and satisfaction. But I wondered if I was in over my head.

Even if I wanted to, I couldn't put Barney up for adoption. He was so damaged, so afraid of people. *Lord*, I prayed, *tell me what you want me to do with this dog.*

"Barney," I told my charge, "you just need to be loved." I had always believed that love healed all wounds, yet Barney's seemed so deep.

Then came Dane. Not a stray dog, but a little boy. He was a sweet-faced eight-year-old who lived with his family in a nearby apartment. He loved the country, and he longed for the freedom of opening a door and running out into a backyard. He'd also recently lost a cat and he missed it terribly. "Hi, Sharon!" he'd call whenever he saw me on the street with my dogs. He rushed over when he spotted me walking my new dog.

"Don't pet him," I warned.

"What's his name?" Dane asked.

"Barney McCabe," I said. Dane stood still, and let Barney sniff. Barney's tail wagged almost imperceptibly.

Dane began a ritual. When I came home after work, Dane was waiting outside. First we took Ginger and Fonzie for a walk, then we walked Barney. Before long I was letting Dane hold his leash. Back inside the apartment, Dane played with the dogs. He wrestled with Fonzie or played tug-of-war with Ginger. All the while, Barney looked on.

One spring day Dane showed up with a pocketful of dog biscuits. He gave some to the other two dogs, then he looked at me and asked, "May I?"

"Go ahead."

"Barney, sit," he said. Barney obeyed. "Okay, now, here's a dog biscuit. It's for you. Take it." He held the treat out. Barney leaned forward and gobbled it right from his open palm.

Watching the two of them, I couldn't help wondering, *God, is that what you'd planned all along?* Barney was to be Dane's friend. I couldn't have guessed that on Christmas Day, and I certainly couldn't have known the role I would play.

"Good dog," Dane said. And then Barney nuzzled the boy's neck and licked his ear.

Britches the
Blue Heeler

Reldon Bray

Mom, who suffered from congestive heart failure and lived alone, was having another one of her rough days. While I sat with her at her house that afternoon I buried my head in the local newspaper rather than make her expend her energy talking. I turned to the classifieds, hoping to find something worthwhile in the dogs-for-sale section. I needed another dog to help me work the eighty head of cattle my wife, Rose, and I keep on our farm. My eyes flew right to the listing "Blue Heeler for Sale." Also called Australian cattle dogs, blue heelers are ideal ranch workers. They're born to herd, and they do it really well. Ann, the dog we had, was the same breed. I called the number in the ad.

I found out that Britches, a two-year-old, belonged to a boy whose parents had moved into town. Blue heelers need daily exercise and lots of space to run. Britches didn't have that anymore, so the boy's folks had decided to find a better home for the dog rather than coop him up. It was a tough but fair decision. I made arrangements to see the dog, then hung up.

"Sounds like an ideal mate for Ann," I said to Mom. I described Britches.

Mom nodded, then rasped haltingly, "It'll be hard for him to part with that boy, though." She paused to catch her breath. "You know how blue heelers can be one-person dogs."

I looked away. I hated seeing Mom struggle so hard to breathe. Despite the best of care and my constant prayers, each day she seemed a little weaker. Still, she remained cheerful, and I kept telling myself she'd get better soon. "Reldon," she spoke up, "the sooner that dog gets back to work, the better."

Seemed Mom always knew just what to say to me. Though I didn't get why she had to be so bad off, work was something I understood. I promised I'd go check Britches out that day.

When I saw the dog pacing around his little backyard, bluish head held high, I felt sorry for him trapped inside the fence. I made arrangements for the boy and his uncle to bring the dog to my place to see what he could do. The next day I watched Britches follow simple commands, cutting cattle from a small herd and guiding them into holding pens. I bought him on the spot.

After the boy and his uncle drove away, I gave Britches a pat on the head and called him to follow me. Instead, he plopped down on the ground, tucked his head close to his chest and refused to budge. I was barely able to get him to the house.

Eye contact is an important part of training a dog, but Britches refused to look directly at me. Nor would he follow a single command. "That dog doesn't even blink when I call his name," I complained to Mom.

"Poor fellow misses his boy," she said, then urged me to bring Britches to meet her.

"Up!" I commanded Britches that afternoon, trying to get him into the back of my pickup. But he refused to obey, even though I'd seen him follow the same order when given by his boy. Finally, I had to lift the dog onto the pickup's bed, then tie down his leash for fear he'd bolt. In Mom's driveway I unfastened the leash and commanded, "Britches, down!" He went through the plop, tuck, refuse-to-budge routine. I tugged gently on the leash, saying, "Come, Britches." No use. I pulled harder, but he resisted me with all his strength. "Who's training who here?" I snapped at the dog.

I almost had to drag him inside. Mom was sitting on the couch, looking pale and tired. "Come here, Britches," she said, stretching out her arms. He went right over. Her hands were shaking badly, but she still managed to scratch him behind his ears. "What a fine fellow you are!" she praised. Britches wagged his tail.

"I'll be darned," I said. "That dog won't even look at me."

"You just have to give him some time, Reldon."

"Well, I've never seen such a stubborn dog," I told her. "He's never going to accept me."

"That dog's got a lot of adjusting to do," she said. "Just keep working with him, Son. He'll come around."

Maybe she's right, I told myself. After all, he does seem to respond to her. I took Britches with me every day when I went to visit Mom. He'd run over to her when she greeted him, then stretch out in front of her, perking up to look right at her face every time she spoke. Still, the only thing he'd do for me was walk through Mom's front door. Mom was real tickled by my frustration, but kept assuring me the dog would come around.

I wondered about that. And I worried about Mom. She was getting so weak that she could only talk for short periods before needing a rest. One day in December, I stopped in front of her spare room. Something struck me as different. Then I realized: This was the first holiday season the room hadn't been crammed with gifts and homemade treats for Mom's friends and family. Now it was too neat, too empty. I turned away quickly and went to fix Mom and me a simple lunch.

After I helped Mom to the table, we sat and bowed our heads. I thought about how many times we'd gone through this ritual together, how few times we might have left. I kept my head down longer than usual after Mom's breathless "Amen" so I wouldn't lose it when I looked at her again.

The rest of that day was quiet. We talked when Mom felt up to it, but mostly we just sat together. I answered the phone a few times. Always it was Mom's friends checking in. After one call I said, "You sure do have a lot of folks praying for you to get well, Mom." I forced a smile, then added, "Including me."

I had to lean close to hear her reply, which was barely a whisper. "Some things you can't change, Son. God doesn't always answer our prayers the way we think he should."

Driving home that day I couldn't get those words out of my head. I gripped the steering wheel so hard my fingers turned white. She has to get better, she just has to. After I parked, I sat in the truck, staring at the mountains. *Oh, Lord, help me*, I prayed. *I know Mom's telling me she's not going to be here forever, but it's so hard to accept that. Help me to come around.*

Britches's barking from the truck bed startled me. I went around to untie his leash. I reached over to scratch him on the head, but he retreated. It was the last straw. Pulling my hand away, I slumped against the truck and wiped my tears with my sleeve.

I had months' worth of unspoken sadness in me, and I don't know how long I stood there crying before I felt a gentle bump against my leg. Britches. He was looking right into my face. His tail wasn't wagging, and his ears lay low, but his eyes locked with mine. "We're quite a pair," I said to the dog. "You lost your master, and I'm losing my mom. What are we going to do?"

It was the first time I'd gotten a good look at his eyes. They seemed to me to be filled with misery and longing. *Is that the way I look to you, God?* I wondered. I stooped to stroke Britches's tense body. "You are without a doubt one of the finest dogs I have ever had the pleasure of meeting," I said softly. When I leaned my cheek against his silky head, he didn't pull away. "Good boy," I whispered. "I know how hard this change is, believe me," I told him. "I'm going to keep working with you. You'll come around." Britches relaxed, and for the first time in weeks, so did I.

Then his tail thumped against the ground. I felt a comforting warmth, despite the biting December wind. "Come on, boy." I headed toward the house. A few paces back, Britches followed.

The next morning I had to move some cattle down to the barn. I got Ann and decided I'd give Britches a shot at it too. At the truck I called, "Up!" and Ann hopped right in. Britches stood his ground. I was disappointed, but I tried not to show it. Instead I knelt beside him and said, "Britches, I know you know what 'up' means. Fine, you're still getting used to me. But from now on, we've got to help each other. Pretty soon you're going to be the finest working dog in the state of Arkansas." His tail thumped a bit more than it had the night before.

I stood. "C'mon, Britches, I know you can do this. Up!" He jumped into the bed of the truck.

By the time we reached the back pasture, both dogs were leaning forward, bright-eyed and eager. I called, "Down!" and they leaped from the truck and raced toward the herd. They circled to get the cows moving, then weaved in and out to round up the stragglers. Britches zigzagged behind one head-strong cow, nipping at her heels, and I thought, *Mom was right. This is going to work out just fine.*

Mom died two months later. For a while I couldn't stand to be around people. By then Britches was always by my side. During the months that followed he was the only earthly comfort I had, and all the more so because of what Mom had said: "He'll come around." And whenever I watched Britches dash across a field to cut off a straggling cow, I found myself coming around too.

Poultrygeist

Jon Katz

Like other friends and loved ones, dogs can mark periods in one's life, boundaries between one time and another.

Julius and Stanley were my dogs during the years when I left behind media companies and big commercial institutions and became a solitary writer. They were by my side when I wrote nearly all my books, articles, and columns. They were around for much of my daughter's childhood. Almost all my ideas germinated or developed while I was walking them. For a socially uneasy man, they provided real companionship; not a replacement for human beings, but a steadfast loving presence. They offered gifts I could never repay.

When a dog like Devon enters your life, your days become so full that it's easy to let the memory of those warm, undemanding creatures fade away. Devon took up space; he made everyone around him take notice. It was a blessing and a curse.

Life with him is a curious mix of love and fun and an intellectual combat that never entirely ends. His is just not a pliant personality.

For instance, a couple of months after Homer arrived, Paula and I came home from a movie to find the refrigerator door standing ajar. Conspicuously missing was the roast chicken I'd bought at the supermarket, encased in a domed plastic tray that was hard to pry open. *Hmmm . . .* someone had goofed and neglected to close the door properly, and someone else had taken full advantage of the goof. I had a fair idea who.

I looked around the kitchen and saw no chicken. I did see Devon scurrying up the stairs so silently I would have missed it if I hadn't glimpsed his disappearing tail. Homer, always stricken at the prospect of trouble, had the panicky look that came on him whenever Devon and I tangled. And by now, I believed Devon was capable of almost any kind of mischief.

Something was definitely afoot. I gave the dining room and family room careful scrutiny. Nothing. But something was sticking out from beneath a black leather chair in the living room. It was the bottom half of the plastic container, but there wasn't a shred of chicken in it.

Crawling around the room, I located the other half underneath the sofa. Neither part of the container had been chewed or torn, simply opened with the dexterity that usually requires an opposable thumb.

I yelled to Paula in her office. "Is Devon up there with you?"

"Yes," she said, pleased. "He came up to visit me, which he hardly ever does when you're around. He looks nervous."

It took me a few days to piece it together, and even then I wasn't sure what had happened. The chicken had weighed several pounds. How could a dog, even finding the refrigerator providentially open, pull the chicken out, carry it twenty-five feet without dropping it or making a stain, pry open a plastic container, eat every scrap without leaving a trace, then stash the evidence under two different pieces of furniture? It didn't add up, even for legendarily crafty Border collies.

Too many steps, too much calculation. Still, whatever had happened had happened; I could hardly yell at him after the fact. Besides, I still didn't quite believe it.

The chicken's fate, however accomplished, was clear when we took our walk that night. Devon had gorged himself; the weakness in his plan was that with a dog, what goes in soon comes out. From the evidence, Homer probably hadn't gotten a morsel. Knowing that eating poultry bones could be dangerous, I called Dr. King, who told me to watch for any bleeding. And to be sure to close the fridge when I left the house.

Two days later, I bought some meatballs in a similar container for lunch and put them in the refrigerator. And, yes, I made sure the door was closed and slid a kitchen chair in front of it for good measure. When I came up from my office an hour later, the chair was askew, the refrigerator open, the meatballs gone. I found the container underneath the black leather chair. Devon was edging toward the stairs.

This time, I roared, picking up the container and yelling "No!" Charging after Devon, I tripped over the carpet, sprawling to the floor. Homer shrieked. Devon was nowhere to be found.

I e-mailed Deanne. Had she ever known a Border collie to open the refrigerator? "Only one," she replied. "Devon's mom."

This was a whole new level of trouble, something that would drive me mad. I hated the idea of guarding food from a sneaky dog.

What particularly bothered me was that Devon didn't really care much about food.

He picked and nibbled at his own, hardly ever finishing it at one sitting, sometimes forgetting about it altogether. We'd known for months that he could open the kitchen cabinet that held the big sacks of dog food. But he never actually ate it when we were away. Dog food? Where was the challenge in that?

This stunt, similarly, had little to do with hunger. It was either pique at being left—my bet—or one of those games Border collies come up with to occupy themselves when they're bored. Opening a sealed refrigerator with your nose (I guess) and then opening a snapped-together plastic container (How? I couldn't imagine)—now that was fun.

I was upset. Devon had been doing so well. There was a malevolent quality to this, I thought.

Paula, on he other hand, was rather impressed. She started talking about hiding the car keys, the credit cards, and computer passwords.

Another fight. I was a veteran by now, with many scars, battle ribbons, and stories to tell of my campaigns.

I bought some turkey burgers at the market, tucked them into the fridge, put my coat on, and went out into the backyard.

Wishing I had a video camera—a collie-cam—that would record and reveal exactly how this theft was going down, I stood perfectly still, my ear to the door. A couple of minutes later, I heard what I thought was a very light thud, and charged inside.

There, sitting on the floor of the family room, was the popped-open container, the turkey burgers still inside. The refrigerator door stood open. Homer was paralyzed with fear, and Devon had beat a tactical retreat.

How dare he? I girded for battle, until a light bulb went off in my head and I reminded myself of certain verities. Paula was right. It was both amusing and impressive. And he's a Border collie. He's Devon, the Professor Moriarty of dogs. If you love him, accept him. This is part of life with him.

I laughed and sat down on the floor. "Hey, boy," I said to Homer, who rushed over, immensely relieved and full of kisses. "C'mon down, Devon, you creep," I yelled upstairs. "It's okay." Devon came roaring down a second later, knocking Homer out of the way and landing in my lap. We hugged for a while, the bewildered but overjoyed Homer trying to get into the act.

What can you do but laugh and sigh and accept the new nature of things? It wasn't easy, because of all the impatience and anger and frustration in my life, and because I so missed Julius and Stanley and their peaceful reliability. But it was necessary, because I was so crazy about this deranged dog.

"You know what?" I said. "For all the ingenuity, you deserve the burger." I took it out of the leakproof plastic, put one turkey patty in Homer's bowl and one in Devon's. Homer scarfed it up gleefully, but Devon didn't touch his, glancing at it with disdain. The thrill was purely in the hunt.

The Pit Bull and the Peke-a-poo

Suzanne Vaden

J ake!" my husband called out.

"Jake!" I shouted. "Jake, where are you, boy?"

Our voices echoed in the bitter wind whistling through the hickory trees. As the light was draining from the December sky, we tramped through the wet leaves and grass stretching behind our house. "Jake!" I yelled, squinting at the thick woods out back, woods filled with foxes, owls and hawks, hungry predators all. And Jake, a mere five furry pounds, would be easy prey.

"Maybe he'll come back on his own," said my husband.

"Jim, he gets lost in our back seat."

Jake was definitely an indoor dog, a puddle of spilled cream with two raisin eyes and a black button nose. All of our previous dogs had been large, rangy outdoor animals, the kind that take you for a walk, but when our last one, an English shepherd named Sass, got run over on the road in front of our house, I swore, no more. It was just too hard to keep an eye on an active outdoor dog. Sass had been part of our family, and it had taken many months for us to get over his death. I couldn't bear to have my heart broken again. I'd rather not have a dog than risk getting hurt.

Jake had belonged to our daughter, Crystal. The first time we met, he practically did back flips. "What breed is he?" Jim had said suspiciously. He wasn't half the size of our cat.

"A Peke-a-poo," Crystal said. "Half-Pekingese, half-poodle."

A dog like that, I found myself thinking, would be perfectly happy indoors. Then Crystal had her first baby. An infant and a dog proved too much for her. Would Jim and I take Jake? I hesitated, remembering my vow. Yet Jake was so delightful, and I missed having a dog. *All right, Lord, this is your idea. But I need you to help protect Jake, and to protect me. I don't want to go through what we went through with Sass. I'm trusting you.*

We set up Jake's bed in the spare bedroom. He and our cat, Miss Kitty, got along just fine, and he soon had every window scouted out for squirrel watching. He studied our habits like a detective. We couldn't put our shoes on without him getting up on his hind paws and begging to come with us. He'd sit on a blanket in the back seat of the car, front paws on the window ledge as he looked out and occasionally commented on the passing scene with a perfunctory woof. About the only place he didn't come with us was church. Sunday mornings he'd eye me lazily as I donned my good clothes, then he'd trot back to his bed.

Outside we didn't take our eyes off him. Once, the big hunting dog next door picked Jake up in his mouth like a rag doll. Jake was unharmed—and unchastened—but we never let him out on his own. I couldn't trust where his high spirits would take him.

Jake had been with us about a year when new neighbors moved in, a young couple with three children. *Perfect*, I thought as I watched the bikes, bats and toys come out of the moving van. *Kids for Jake to play with*. That was before I saw the two ominously large dog pens.

The couple came over to introduce themselves. "Hi, I'm J. R. Wooley," the man said. "This is my wife, Sherry." J. R. leaned down to pet Jake. "He's a cute one. Our kids are used to bigger dogs."

"What kind?" Jim asked.

J. R. and Sherry glanced at each other. "Uh, actually we raise them," J. R. said. "They're pit bulls."

Pit bulls! The man might as well have said grizzly bears. Pit bulls! Jake would be an hors d'oeuvre for them.

"I know what you're thinking," J. R. went on. "These dogs have gotten a bum rap. If they're raised right they turn out fine, same as any dog. I'd trust any of my pits with this little guy here." *Not on your life*, I thought. "Anyway," he said, "we keep 'em penned."

The Wooleys turned out to be wonderful neighbors. I just couldn't get used to their dogs. I'd see them in their pens and shudder. Their eyes were dark and impassive and their tails so stubby it was hard to know when they were wagging them. They stalked around like prizefighters in a ring, muscles bulging.

One day J. R. invited us over. "Bring Jake with you. I've got someone y'all need to meet." A wiggling pit bull pup not much bigger than a Peke-a-poo. "I figured Jake and Mason should get to know each other. He's got great bloodlines. He's going to be my best dog." The two sniffed at each other, Jake's tail wagging. In no time at all, they were playing.

Their friendship was sealed. Like a little kid looking for a playmate, Mason would appear at our storm door, pawing at the glass. "Jake, your friend is here!" I'd say. Jake would come running. Outside they dashed after each other in dizzy circles under my watchful eye. They roughhoused under the trees, and played tug of war with sticks. One glimpse of a squirrel sent them on a mad chase. Yet I never dared leave them alone. Once Mason reached his full growth, Jake was no bigger than a chew toy next to him.

Jim and I asked the Wooley kids to come over and take care of Jake while we were away on vacation. Jake managed to convince our neighbors that he'd actually be happier staying with them. It was like a sleepover, Jake curled up right next to Mason, their water dishes side by side. The only thing he didn't do with Mason was explore the woods behind our homes. That was strictly off limits for Jake.

After four years, the Wooleys had to move. "Jake sure is going to miss Mason," I told J. R.

"We're going to miss Jake," he said. All that fall, Jake stared out the window, searching for his buddy. He waited by the storm door for the pit bull's paw. Chasing squirrels, he kept checking for Mason at his heels. Finally, Jake resigned himself to having just Jim and me for company. That cold December afternoon he clipped along at our ankles, his fur rippling in the frigid air as we carried some things out back.

"I'm going in now, Jim," I said. "I've got to drive to town for some shopping."

"Okay," he called from the shed.

In Wal-Mart, my cell phone rang. Jim's voice was panicky. "Suzanne, is Jake with you?"

"No. I thought he was with you."

"I can't find him anywhere," Jim said. I rushed home. Jim was in the driveway.

"I've scoured the yard, checked under the porch, everywhere I can think of." We headed out back. My gaze fell on the tangled wilderness beyond the shed. Jake would never find his way home from there. I paused for a minute and closed my eyes. *Lord, where can he be?*

Immediately, I thought of our old neighbors. Mason! I punched in the Wooleys' number on my cell phone. *Please, God, let someone be home.*

"We'll be there as fast as we can," J. R. said. In less than fifteen minutes the headlights of J. R.'s truck pierced the dark. Mason jumped out the door, sniffing the yard. J. R. clipped a leash on him. "We'll head into the woods," he said. Jim and I went in different directions, knocking on neighbors' doors, searching yards. We called Crystal and her family, and they came and helped in the search.

Three hours later, at 10:00 P.M., we met back at the house, exhausted and defeated, our boots sodden from the damp. The temperature had dropped into the twenties. "I've got to get home now," J. R. said. "I'll leave Mason on your deck. He can take the cold. Let's see what he'll do on his own. If Jake's out there, Mason might be the only shot he's got."

Jake had been missing since five, a long time in this brutal cold. I was afraid that if Mason did find Jake it would be too late. I grabbed the biggest, warmest blanket I could find and laid it out on the deck, along with a full bowl of food. "Come on, Mason," Jim called. Mason trotted out. Ignoring the food, he cocked his head. Suddenly he took off, *thump, thump, thump*, down the steps and disappeared into the moonless night.

I paced the kitchen. I prayed. I went to the storm door. Just the darkness and the wind. Then I remembered the prayer I'd said when we adopted Jake. *God, I need you to help protect him.* Hadn't God already protected Jake from a big hunting dog? Maybe it was time to let go of my fears and let God take over. *Okay, God, you gave us Jake and you know how much we love him. I trust you to take care of him now, and of me.*

Our clock chimed eleven. The next thing I heard was *thump, thump, thump*. I threw open the storm door. There on the deck, huddled like a wet, muddy toy next to Mason's muscular legs, was Jake. I knelt and threw my arms around them both.

As soon as we got the dogs wrapped in blankets by the heater, I called J. R. "Mason found him! Jake's home!"

"I knew we could count on Mason," he said. I looked over at the dogs, curled up next to each other, and thought about how you can never really lose what you love when you entrust it to God. He takes care of all of us—pit bulls, Peke-a-poos, and especially their ever anxious owners.

Help and Healing

from Unlikely Heroes

Arnie's Mission

Eunice Merritt

I had been known to do some impetuous things, but this? There I was, lying on my sofa, recovering from back surgery—or trying to, anyway. The nagging pain and inability to get around had left me feeling pretty low. The last thing that I needed was a new dog. Especially an excitable, high-maintenance puppy.

Sure, I was a dog lover—a big-dog lover—Golden retrievers and Labs, not small yappy types. If I were even to consider a new dog, it would have to be a female, older and housebroken. But my friend Connie convinced me to take home an eight-week-old, caramel-colored, male toy poodle. "You need someone to cheer you up," Connie said.

"Not this puppy," I protested. "All he's going to be is a lot of work. I don't have the energy."

"C'mon, look at him," she coaxed. "How can you resist that face?" I found myself looking into raisin-dark eyes that looked right back at me with what I could've sworn was a twinkle.

Connie left, saying she'd call in a few days and take him back if I wanted. The puppy leaped onto the sofa and cuddled on my chest. Pretty soon he was dozing, his little body as warm as a fluffy down comforter. I had to admit, a big dog couldn't do that.

Later he woke and scampered down and picked up the corner of the rug, rolling himself in it like a burrito. I laughed out loud, and I hadn't laughed in a long time. "Okay, little guy," I said, "maybe you can stay."

I figured I might as well give him a name if he was going to stick around. I chose Arnie, short for Arnold Palmer, my favorite golfer. Over the next few days Arnie and I got to know each other. When I took him out, I found that he was smart and trainable. He came quickly to his name. Our walks did me good too, giving my spirits a lift as the pain from surgery eased. By the time Connie called and asked if I wanted her to take Arnie back, I exclaimed, "Not on your life!"

As my slow shuffle progressed to an easy stride, our walks became longer. Arnie learned to wait for me when crossing the street. And he'd stay by my side if there was another dog near, all eight pounds of him ready to leap to my defense. He wanted to pick up every stick in the neighborhood. Sometimes I had to burst out laughing when he dragged along a branch three or four times his size. He might've been a toy poodle, but he thought he was a full-size retriever.

I had been back to work for several months when my company announced it was transferring me to Boston for two years. My heart sank as I realized I couldn't take Arnie. It would be difficult to find an apartment that allowed pets, and there would be no backyard for him to play in. My mother agreed to keep him in Cleveland until I returned, and I hugged them both goodbye. "I'll be back to see you soon, Arnie," I promised, burying my face in his soft fur.

In Boston I found a nice brownstone apartment in the Back Bay. The neighborhood was filled with fine nineteenth-century homes and upscale boutiques. Elegant . . . but intimidating. Kind of like the people. If I hadn't had to ask Joan and John, the couple upstairs, where to buy groceries, where to get gas, and where to park, I doubt I would've met anyone those first few months.

On a blustery April evening when the wind brought some branches down, I was telling Joan about what a field day Arnie would have picking up sticks.

"Why don't you bring him out here?" Joan asked matter-of-factly.

"Do you think it would be all right with the other people in the building?"

"As long as he's well behaved," she said. "Let the others meet him and see."

So on my next trip to Cleveland I picked Arnie up and brought him back to Boston with me. The bustle of Logan Airport hardly fazed him, and during the taxi ride to the Back Bay he kept his nose out the window, sniffing eagerly all the way. He got out in front of our brownstone and trotted up the steps like it was home.

Other people in the building seemed to approve of him; at least no one complained. "Your hair's the same color as mine," Joan told Arnie one day in the elevator. She scratched him under the chin, then looked up at me. "How old is he?"

"Arnie just turned one on April sixth."

She laughed. "That's my birthday too!"

I took him on long walks every morning and evening. All sorts of people stopped to pet Arnie, and soon everybody in the neighborhood knew him . . . and me. I'd go out for groceries and people would shout, "Hey, Arnie!" I'd sit on a park bench and find myself striking up a conversation with a total stranger who admired my dog. One day Arnie scampered up to an old woman in a wheelchair. She picked him up and started petting him.

"I hope that's all right," I said to the nurse who was pushing the wheelchair.

"She hasn't smiled like this in days," the nurse said. I wasn't the only one Arnie had an instinct for cheering up.

One evening Joan invited both Arnie and me upstairs for coffee. As soon as we sat down, Arnie leaped into her lap.

"Arnie, down!" I said.

"No, no, it's fine," she said, scratching his ears.

Then I noticed tears in Joan's eyes. "Is everything all right?" I asked.

Her voice was soft, but her words cut me to the quick. "I have breast cancer," she said. "I have to have chemotherapy."

I didn't know what to say. "Is there anything I can do?" I managed to ask. Joan shook her head. I prayed, *Lord, if there's any way I can help her, let me know.*

That December when I was going back to Cleveland for Christmas, Joan offered to look after Arnie. "Are you sure?" I asked, worried that it would be too much for her, considering her treatments. "It'll be fun," she insisted.

John agreed. "I think it will help her as much as it will you."

As soon as I was back at the brownstone after Christmas I called Joan. "Did everything go okay with Arnie?"

"Of course. He was great company."

"I'll come right up and get him."

"There's no hurry. I'm sure you're tired after your flight. You can pick him up tomorrow." I decided he couldn't have been too much of a bother.

After that, Joan volunteered to take Arnie out at lunchtime while I was at the office. I started bringing him to see Joan every morning after his walk. Gradually I let him stay there all day. "Think of this as doggie day care," Joan told me.

"I hope it's not too much," I said to John when I ran into him in the hall.

"Absolutely not. She shows him off to friends, and even takes him to the hospital to see other patients. Arnie keeps her mind off being sick. He's been a godsend."

I knew the feeling.

By then Arnie had developed a social life that was beyond my reckoning. People I'd never even seen before greeted him by name. Once he received an invitation in the mail to attend someone's fortieth birthday party. "To Arnie Merritt," it said, and then almost as an afterthought, "and guest."

One weekend that summer John and Joan took him to a friend's cottage on Cape Cod. "He was such a good guest," Joan said. "Our friends said he's welcome to stay anytime." I felt like a proud parent.

That summer, too, the doctors declared that Joan's cancer was in remission. We had a party to celebrate and Arnie was, as usual, the center of attention. Not long after, when Joan and John went to buy a new car, they asked to take Arnie with them. "We want to make sure he likes it." Sure enough, they picked a Jeep Cherokee with a golden-brown interior that matched Arnie's coat.

All too soon, my two years in Boston were up. I couldn't believe how much I had loved living there. I was going to miss my new friends, especially John and Joan. *How can I thank them for everything they've done?* I wondered. An idea crept up on me. As much as I tried to ignore it, it stayed with me. I prayed and prayed about it, and it became clearer.

Finally I went upstairs to see Joan. Arnie trotted into her apartment ahead of me. When Joan and I sat down on the sofa, he climbed onto her lap.

"You know, Joan, I'm going to be leaving in a few weeks."

"John and I are really going to miss having you right downstairs," she said. "I'm going to miss you, too, Arnie," Joan added, stroking his head, and Arnie leaned into her touch. "He's gotten me through some tough times."

"I know," I said. "That's why I want you to keep him."

Joan's eyes widened. "You don't mean that. You can't . . . " Her voice trailed off.

"I do mean it. Arnie saw me through my back surgery and my move to Boston. I love him, but I know you love him too. And I know this is where he belongs now."

"Eunice, thank you," Joan said. "This means more than I can say." Arnie gave a happy bark, as if he understood.

Right before I left Boston, I moved Arnie and his bed and his dog dish and toys upstairs. Several months later I learned that Joan's cancer was back. I called her often from Cleveland on the pretext of asking about Arnie, but really to see how she was. It didn't surprise me to hear her say, "Eunice, I honestly don't know what I'd do without him." It was John who told me that when Joan had to go into the hospital for treatment, Arnie was a regular during visiting hours.

The doctors informed Joan and John that she would lose her battle to cancer. Joan wanted to spend her last days at home, so a hospital bed was set up in their apartment. Arnie wouldn't leave her side. When she slept, he curled up right next to her. Late one night Arnie jumped on John's bed, and John knew that the end had come.

After the funeral, John called. We spoke about Joan. He cleared his throat.

"Eunice, I want to thank you for Arnie. You don't know what a difference he's made. He really made Joan smile. And . . . well, he makes me smile. I need that. Especially now."

What was it that John had called Arnie back when they—and we—had first become friends? A godsend. It was true. Only God could have foreseen how this little caramel-colored poodle had a heart big enough to draw people together and bring each of us the healing we needed.

Somehow I had the feeling that his work for Arnie wasn't over yet.

Calling
Doctor Trilby

John Sherrill

There was one thing dog trainer Jeanne Gurnis wished she could have done for her mother before she died. "Mother was in the intensive care unit, and she kept asking to see Corky, her dog," Jeanne recalled. "But the hospital wouldn't hear of it. All I could bring her were photos. She had me prop the pictures on her nightstand, so Corky would be the first one to greet her when she woke up, just like at home." Still, Jeanne couldn't help wondering how much more her mother's last days could have been brightened if she'd been able to hug her beloved Corky.

So when a local hospital, Westchester Medical Center, just north of New York City, approached her about starting a pet-therapy program—where specially trained animals would visit patients—Jeanne knew she had to give it a try. "This is only a test," the staff warned her. "We'll have to see if pet therapy really does the patients any good."

The spring of 1999, Jeanne and Trilby, a bright-eyed little corgi who'd been certified through Therapy Dogs International, became the first volunteer pet-therapy team at the hospital. The staff's initial concerns about infection diminished when they learned Trilby had regular checkups, and was bathed and groomed before each visit. And resistance melted away entirely as patients' morale and recovery rate improved measurably after Trilby stopped in to see them.

That December a doctor called Trilby to the intensive care unit to see a patient who seemed beyond medical help. Brain-injured in a car accident, Babs Barter had been in a coma for three weeks. Her husband said she loved dogs, so her doctor decided to try Trilby.

Jeanne knew it was a long shot; patients needed to interact with an animal to benefit. As she and Trilby headed into the ICU, Jeanne prayed, as she often did before a tough assignment, *Father, please guide this visit. Thy will be done.*

Babs was on a ventilator, her motionless body bristling with wires and tubes. With the doctor, head nurse, and Babs's husband looking on, Jeanne and Trilby went up to her. "Hello, I'm Jeanne Gurnis. I've brought someone to see you."

Jeanne lifted Trilby onto the bed. "I heard you're a dog lover," Jeanne said. No response. She put Babs's limp hand on the dog's back. "Trilby is a Pembroke Welsh corgi. Want to pet her?"

Still no response. Jeanne kept talking. Twenty minutes passed with no hint of awareness from Babs. "You know, if you don't hold Trilby she might fall off the bed." No reaction. *Lord, what should I do now?* Jeanne wondered.

That's when Trilby took charge. Ever so slowly the little corgi inched closer to Babs's still body. It was a stretch to suppose that a dog—even one as smart as Trilby—understood what Jeanne was getting at. But then Babs's husband exclaimed, "Look . . . look!"

Jeanne saw it too. Almost imperceptibly, the fingers of the comatose woman moved. "Trilby likes that," Jeanne said to Babs. "Why don't you keep petting her?"

Babs's doctor was so delighted he asked Jeanne and Trilby to come by every day. They did, though Babs's response remained too slight to be sure of.

One morning three weeks after their first visit, Jeanne clearly saw Babs move her fingers. It was unmistakable—she was stroking the dog's soft, thick fur! Two weeks later, Jeanne and Trilby watched Babs's eyes flicker open. When Babs was strong enough to transfer to a rehabilitation center, she got permission for Trilby to visit. Soon Babs was doing so well she was able to go home.

Just before Christmas 2000, a box arrived at Jeanne's house, addressed in a firm, clear hand. "To Trilby Gurnis."

Inside was a huge batch of fresh dog biscuits, and a note from Babs Barter. "Baked by me for Trilby, who saved my life. Thanks for the first-class care."

Punkie's Secret

Linda D. Baxter

Snowflakes swirled past my face as I shut and locked the back door. "Wait for Mommy, Lesley," I called to my six-year-old daughter, who was crunching through the frozen yard, already several inches thick with snow. I was a little surprised kindergarten hadn't been canceled—the weather reports said we were in for quite a storm. But Lesley's school was only a block and a half away, thank goodness. It wouldn't take long to go pick her up if the weather got any worse.

I took Lesley's mittened hand in mine and headed down the sidewalk. As we passed the Roths' house next door Lesley searched the yard, especially around the snow-covered doghouse. "It's too cold for Punkie to be out today," I said.

Most days Lesley stopped to pet the Roths' German shepherd on the way to and from school. I remembered Lesley coming home from her very first day of kindergarten; she ran up to Punkie to tell her all about it. "Guess what happened at school, Punkie," Lesley cried before cupping her hand to her mouth and whispering in Punkie's pointed ear.

"What's that you're saying?" Mr. Roth asked, pretending to listen in.

"It's a secret," Lesley said. "Between Punkie and me." Whatever it was, Punkie never told a soul.

I envied Punkie, all warm and cozy inside, as I passed the Roths' on my way back home. The wind had picked up, and the snow was beginning to fall even heavier than before. I flicked on the kitchen radio to monitor the weather reports. Sure enough, an hour later I heard the announcement I'd been expecting—because of the blizzard, Lesley's school would close at noon. I pulled on my still-wet boots and coat and stepped out the back door. By then the drifts were up to my knees, making each step a struggle. "Do all the children know how they're getting home?" I asked Lesley's teacher when I finally arrived.

"We're making sure now," she answered. "Don't worry, we'll sit tight till they're all taken care of. You'd better start home, though. It's piling up fast."

I took Lesley's hand, and we hurried to the school door. The snow blocked the door, and I had to push hard to open it. A gust of wind whistled through and nearly knocked Lesley down. *How will we manage?* I wondered, suddenly realizing that snowdrifts to my knees would reach Lesley's waist. No way could I walk and carry her, even the block and a half.

It might as well have been miles. Lesley sank up to her middle and made just the slightest headway with little hops rather than steps. Halfway down the block her cheeks were cherry red from the wind that pushed her back as the snow sucked her down. "Can't you carry me, Mommy?" she said, starting to cry.

"I wish I could, Lesley," I said, trying not to cry myself. "But Mommy can't walk too well either." I wiped her eyes and gave her a kiss. "We'll make it. We'll just take one step at a time." We struggled on. We'd been walking for at least thirty minutes and hadn't even reached our street. At least, I didn't think we had.

Lesley's legs gave out and she fell face-first in the snow. I bent down and gathered her into my arms. "Are we home yet?" she asked, too exhausted even to cry anymore.

"Almost," I promised. But when I stood up, panic gripped me. I had no idea where we were. Every direction I turned, all I could see was snow. I took a tentative step, then drew back. "Lesley, we need to ask for help." I took her in my arms, trying to shield her from the wind. "Dear Lord, help us find our way home." I lifted my head, searching for something that might signal the way. I saw movement in the thick whiteness. A dark shape clambered over the snow, heading straight for us. "Punkie!" I cried, hardly believing she was real.

Lesley twisted out of my arms and hugged Punkie, who gave her a big sloppy dog kiss in return. She took Punkie's collar in one hand and grabbed my hand with the other. "Take us home, Punkie," Lesley cried happily. Punkie leaped forward, pulling us with her.

After only a few steps, Lesley and I had to stop to catch our breath. Punkie barked encouragement. She was right. Best to keep moving. We followed Punkie blindly, trusting her instincts to get us home. An hour and a half after leaving the school, we finally arrived at our own backyard gate. Lesley threw her arms around Punkie and gave her a kiss. "You go on home now," she said. "It's too cold for you to be outside!"

Punkie barked once more and headed straight across the yard. I had no doubt she'd get there safe and sound. I popped Lesley straight into a hot bath before calling the Roths to tell them about our dramatic rescue. "I'm surprised Punkie was even outside," I said.

"That's the strangest thing," Mrs. Roth said. "You see, Punkie was inside sleeping, when she suddenly jumped up and started barking. She just wouldn't stop until we let her out. When she didn't come back, we called and called for her, but it was well over an hour before she came in, shook off the snow and collapsed, totally exhausted. But how could she have known you two were in trouble?"

"I think," I said, "somebody told her." But whoever it was, Punkie never told a soul.

Dripper
Saves the Day

Stuart Reininger

O ne of the best things about living on a boat is that it's just me. No snooping doorman, no kids playing ball on my front steps, no neighbors blasting loud music. I love it. So much so that I work as a yacht deliverer. I'm on the water almost all the time, and that suits me fine.

I used to go south in the winter, but one December a spell of foul weather changed my plans. It looked like my own boat, *Furthermore*, would be staying put in New Jersey. Grumbling as I hauled some supplies down the dock one night during a blizzard, I saw a floppy-eared puppy with the face of a hung-over bloodhound and the stubby legs of a terrier. He was the size and color of a beagle, shivering and soaking wet. I'd seen that "Heinz 57" sniffing around the docks all summer, begging tourists for scraps.

"What are you doing here?" I said as I opened the hatch. "Whoa!" I almost fell backward as the dog darted between my legs. He rushed into the boat and headed straight to my quarters, where he jumped right up on the bunk.

"Get off of that!" I screamed. The mongrel rolled around, drying himself off on my blankets. He gave me a look

I could only describe as grateful. "All right, pal. C'mon." I grabbed his ratty leather collar and dragged him to the door to throw him out. Snow blew through the open hatch, and into the cabin. The blizzard was raging at full force.

You can't put him out in this, I thought. I let go of his collar and he took off, leaving puddles in his wake.

"No! Not in my bunk again you, you . . . dripper! Get over there." I pointed to a quarter berth that I used for stowage. To my surprise he tucked his tail between his legs and padded right over to where I pointed. "There's hope for you yet, you dripper. That is, at least until I can get rid of you."

And I really did try to get rid of him. But no one responded to the "found dog" leaflets I put up. Meanwhile the winter just got nastier. I couldn't bring myself to throw the dog out. "Well, Dripper," I said one day, "looks like you're stuck with that name for as long as I'm stuck with you." My initial thoughts that he might be, at the very least, a decent watchdog quickly went overboard. He cowered in a corner whenever anyone approached the boat. Then, once the person was aboard, the dog would rub up against his legs until he was petted.

It seemed impossible at first to boat-break him, but once Dripper got the idea, he only wanted to go out in the early mornings. He howled incessantly until I woke up. I'd stumble out with him for a groggy walk. At least the fresh air did me good—even after a bath, Dripper stank to high heaven. But those bad qualities started to grow on me. I don't know if I would ever describe myself as lonely, but there were times when I was more alone than I wanted to be. Anyway, the dog certainly had personality. As much as I hated to admit it, it was nice to have another living creature onboard.

I'd always believed that all God's creatures had a purpose—until Dripper came along. Every time I left Dripper alone, I'd come home to find that in my absence he had gnawed some more varnished wood—an unforgivable sin on a classic wooden sailboat. When I was done yelling at him, he'd slink over and wait for me to pet him.

One night, while scratching behind his mangy ears, I wondered how I'd gotten stuck with him. Words from the book of Job came to mind: "Which of all of these does not know that the hand of the Lord has done this . . . ?"

If you wanted to send me a dog, Lord, couldn't you have found a better one?

About all Dripper was good for was those predawn walks. I'd come to enjoy them. Seemed like Dripper and I were the only ones awake, pacing the docks and waiting to watch the sunrise.

Still, I was counting the days until the warm weather would bring the tourists back. One of those families would surely take Dripper off my hands.

But that day was a long way off. It was one of the worst winters I could remember in New Jersey. Even two electric heaters weren't enough to keep the boat warm. I had to dig my old kerosene heater out of storage.

Burning kerosene could use up all the oxygen in a small place like my cabin without proper ventilation. But I figured it wouldn't be a problem as long as I remembered to crack open a hatch when using the heater.

The heater kept us toasty. And the way Dripper walked in little circles in front of it made me laugh.

One night in February the snow was falling hard again. Big, thick, wet flakes packed the ground, the kind of snow kids love for snowballs. When I went to bed it was still coming down, packing against *Furthermore*'s hatchway. Dripper was already in his berth. I gave him a few pats and fell asleep, grateful for the warmth in my cabin.

Sometime during the night I was wakened by a strange thud. I tried to open my eyes, but the lids felt so heavy. I could barely focus. I managed to make out Dripper lying on the floor. *Wonder what that dumb dog knocked over. Probably wants to go out.* I put my head back on the pillow. *I'm not getting up. Let him start howling.* I drifted off for a while. Then I felt a sharp pain in my ankle.

Sitting up, I noticed Dripper motionless at the foot of the bed. I was shocked to see his teeth clamped on my ankle. *Dripper bit me?* I fell back into bed. *Why am I sweating so much?* I wondered. I felt queasy and couldn't catch a breath. I rolled out of my bunk and landed on my hands and knees. I felt so tired, so heavy. *What's going on?* I tried to stand, but didn't have the strength. I pulled my ankle free of Dripper's jaws. *I need air.* I had to crawl through the cabin. It felt like I was swimming through molasses. *Got to make it to the hatch. . . .*

I passed by Dripper, who was still unconscious. His teeth were stained with my blood, his eyes closed. I threw my weight against the hatch. It wouldn't budge. I tried it again, but I couldn't catch a breath. I slammed my shoulder against the hatch. It flew open, and cold air rushed into the cabin as if it were filling a vacuum. Falling forward into the snow-covered cockpit, I gasped for air. *What happened? The heater! The hatch must've fallen shut. Dripper!*

I raced back below. Dripper was lying in the same spot. He wasn't breathing. *God, please don't let him die,* I prayed, feeling like some kid in a Lassie movie. I dragged him out into the cockpit. He didn't move a muscle. I pushed down on his chest in short bursts. No response. *Please, Lord, I beg you, don't take him. I love this dog. I need him. He saved my life.* I pushed down on his chest again. Nothing. Dripper was gone. I collapsed in the snow and sobbed. I had tried so hard to get rid of Dripper, only to realize how much I needed him. *Lord, I'm sorry. He was your gift to me.*

At first I thought it was a wet sea breeze, but no, it was a lick on my arm. *Dripper!* He gave a weak wag of his tail. I scooped him up and carried him below. To my bunk. After bandaging my ankle, I got into bed next to Dripper. I held him close, keeping him warm all night.

The next morning I woke with my arms still wrapped around the mutt. I inhaled his familiar musty smell, and in return he slobbered my face with kisses. During our walk on the docks later, the rest of that verse from Job came back to me: "In his hand is the life of every living thing and the breath of all mankind." Yes, indeed, God had a plan when he sent me Dripper.

Marmie

Betsy MacDonald

From the day she was born, our Great Dane, Marmalade, couldn't abide being tied up or penned in. But that was the law where we lived in Connecticut. "Marmie," I'd scold her gently, "the dog warden was here again today to complain about you." She'd just sit head held high, dark eyes gazing straight at me as if to say, "You and the warden both know I have important work to do."

Of course she wasn't thinking that, but it seemed Marmie knew she'd been put on this earth to do more than eat dog food and sleep in the shade all day. For instance, one of our neighbors was a retired man who'd recently had open-heart surgery. Daily exercise was part of his recuperation program, so every morning he went for a walk, and every morning Marmie took off to accompany him. In the afternoon, Marmie sat and waited for our son, Ryan, and some of the other kids to get off the school bus. Then she'd walk them home. It was as though she understood that people need protection, or sometimes just plain old companionship, and her heart was full of love for them—especially for Ryan.

Marmie definitely had personality: it wasn't long before she started carrying around one of Ryan's old teddy bears.

Soon people all over town knew her. How could they not notice Marmie? After all, she strolled around with the dignity of an aristocrat and the grace of a deer; the markings on her face made it look like she was wearing a mask; and she always had that teddy bear in her mouth.

One morning Marmie returned from her neighborhood patrol with a doll in her mouth instead. "Where'd you get that?" I asked. "And what happened to your teddy?" Ryan piped in.

Later that day a neighbor called. "Marmie's bear turned up in my yard," she said, "and one of my daughter's dolls is missing."

"So that's where it came from. I'm so sorry," I said. "I'll bring the doll right back."

Marmie traded her bear for things so often that people got used to her barter system. In fact, sometimes we'd pull into the driveway and see the flag up on the mailbox. Inside the box would be the stuffed bear, and standing halfway down the drive with her tail wagging would be Marmie, showing off the new prize she'd tucked in her mouth.

Eventually my husband and I started calling Marmie's daily finds her "gifts from heaven." From the proud look on her face, it seemed she thought that whatever it was she brought home—a bone, a ball, a shoe—had come from some source higher than people.

We never got tired of seeing that expression on Marmie's face, though I must admit we got more than our share of visits from the dog warden. So in 1987, when our family moved to

Virginia, we looked for property that didn't have any leash laws. We found the perfect place in Spotsylvania County—twenty-five open acres lined by a vast pine forest. Marmie would be free to roam, and have more space than ever in which to do it.

We spent that summer building our new home at the back of our property, right by a large pond. It must have been a day in mid-July when we first noticed Marmie standing at the edge of the woods, barking questioningly. After dinner that night she left her bear in Ryan's safekeeping and headed into the trees with some scraps of meat left over from her dinner. "I wonder what that's all about?" I asked Bob.

"Oh, you know Marmie. She's not one to chow down all at once. She's probably just burying it there and she'll go back for it sometime when she's hungry."

Then, in August, Marmie went into the woods with her teddy and came trotting back without him. That time, though, she had no "gift from heaven" in her mouth. That's not like her, I thought. Over the course of the month, Marmie again showed some unusual behavior: She would disappear into the woods and start howling. One day, Bob and I heard Marmie howl, and then a weak bark in response. "Must be a stray, or a hunting dog that got lost," Bob guessed. "Marmie probably found her."

"There she is!" I said, pointing to the spot where Marmie always entered and exited the forest. Our Great Dane stopped and turned, as if to introduce her newest "gift from heaven." A small beagle staggered out from behind her and collapsed to the ground.

"What did you bring home now, Marmie?" Bob said.

He walked cautiously toward the beagle, with me close behind. The dog couldn't have been more than a year old. Her ears were shredded from briers, she was covered with ticks and her body had wasted away to practically nothing. A black leather collar hung loose around her neck. "She must have been lost a very long time," I said.

"Is this where your food's been going, Marmie?" Bob asked, reaching down to stroke our Great Dane's snout. "Okay. If you've given your all for this pup, then so will we."

We tended to the dog's wounds and cleaned her up, got a thick blanket for bedding, then took her to the vet. Ryan held the beagle while the vet examined her. "I don't think she'll last that long," the vet said. Despite his prognosis, during the next few weeks the dog got better. Ryan set out extra food for her every night, and he and Marmie were always coaxing the beagle to eat and walk. And at night Marmie would curl her massive forelegs around the pup, as if to keep her safe and warm while she slept. Soon the puppy had gained enough strength to join Marmie on her daily patrols.

Meanwhile, I tried to find the beagle's owner. I called the SPCA, and I asked around town. No results. Finally I placed an ad in the lost-and-found section of the paper. Two days after the ad ran, our phone rang. "I'm calling about the beagle with the black collar," said a young boy. He started to cry. "I l-l-lost my puppy after Mom was in the hospital." He sobbed so hard I could barely make out his final words: "I'll have Grandpa call you." Then the line went dead.

Not five minutes later the phone rang again. "Ya found a dog?" asked an old man. "My grandson lost his dog. I gave him the pup when his mom was sick. The dog was just five months old when she disappeared from the backyard, the same night my grandson's mom died. I told him God took the pup to keep his mom company. But still he calls every ad that says 'young beagle.'"

"When did the dog disappear?" I asked.

"December," he said gruffly. "No way a young dog could've survived with all the snow we had last winter." He asked where we lived, then said, "Besides, we're in King George, a whole county away. Don't see how the pup could've gotten that far. Though I did make the dog a collar like the one you described in the ad."

"What was the dog's name?" I asked.

"Jeanette. My grandson named her after his mom."

I went to the door and called, "Jeanette! Jeanette!" Though I couldn't be sure, it did seem the puppy stopped playing with Marmie and looked at me. When I told the man on the phone, he made arrangements to come out and see the dog.

The next morning, a pickup truck rattled down our driveway. Bob and I stepped outside as an old man in overalls climbed out of the truck. Marmie and the puppy were playing with Ryan. "Jeanette!" called the man. "Jeanette! If it's you, girl, come!"

The beagle turned her head, raced down the driveway and leaped right into the old man's arms. "Well, young 'un," he said to the puppy, "I thought you were dead after all this time." He climbed into the truck and gently placed the beagle on the seat next to him. Then he turned to us, tears in his eyes. "Got to get her home to the boy. He's been waiting a long time. He never gave up. Guess I shouldn't have either. Thank you." He put the truck in gear and backed out of the driveway.

Our Great Dane stood at attention as the truck turned onto the road. Ryan patted her head. "You did good, Marmie," I said. "You must be a guardian angel for your own kind." She wagged her tail and held her head high, then turned and headed toward the woods. "We know," I said as I watched her disappear into the pines. "You have important work to do."

Dog to the Rescue

Deby Duzan

Summer was coming, and I knew that was bad. My seventeen-year-old daughter, Seleta, hated the summertime. To her summer meant nothing to do, and that meant boredom, which only aggravated her depressive tendencies.

We'd become aware of the problem when she was just ten. She lost interest in everything—school, friends. She didn't even enjoy playing with animals anymore.

It wasn't like her at all. Though at first I chalked it up to growing pains, when she didn't pull out of her funk I began to think it was something more serious. I took her to the doctor. Seleta was diagnosed with depression. Finally we knew what was wrong, but that didn't solve the problem. Seleta was still in so much pain, and it hurt me to see her like that. I wanted to make it all go away, have everything be fine again.

Over the next seven years, I learned that as much as I wanted to cure Seleta, I couldn't. We had some rocky times. As she entered her teens, I wondered if she would ever regain some kind of balance. Seleta hated taking her medication. She said it didn't help, and she didn't like that one of the side effects was weight gain. Kids at school would make fun of her, and she'd stop taking her medication. But the weight stayed on, yet another thing to be depressed about. Then school would let out, summer would come and Seleta would be more depressed than ever. It was a vicious cycle.

When Seleta was down, she wanted nothing other than to sleep. It seemed to be all she ever did. All day, every day. Lord, I'd pray, please help Seleta to feel better. There's got to be some way to make her happy again. I talked to her all the time, trying to find out how she was doing every day. I took her shopping with me and made sure we kept up our weekly night out together. I knew that a trip to the market or a dinner and a movie would force Seleta to get out of the house. It couldn't hurt, I figured, and it might even help. I wouldn't give up on my daughter.

Seleta did have good days, even good weeks or months. But inevitably, as the dark cloud closed in on her once again, she'd slowly sink back into a deep funk. The worst of it came in 1999, right in the middle of her junior year in high school. Three times, Seleta's depression got so bad that she had to check into a behavioral health center, once because of a suicide attempt. I prayed harder than ever, and so did our family and friends.

Eventually her condition stabilized, and she managed to do well in her classes despite the disruptions. But as the semester drew to a close I worried. Would the long summer ahead drag Seleta back down? I was hopeful when she announced she was determined to get a job, just to have something to do, some reason to get out of bed every day.

Seleta found work at a local pet superstore, and started when school let out for the year. Right away she loved her job, and soon I could tell a remarkable change was taking place in my daughter. "I get to talk to lots of different people," she would tell me after work. "And there's all kinds of dogs to pet." Seleta had always loved animals—especially dogs, the bigger the better. Now she was talking about a school in Denver, where she wanted to go after graduation to study to become a veterinary technician. I worried how she'd manage on her own so far from home. Still, I was relieved she seemed to be less gloomy.

One day Seleta called me from the store. "Mom," she said, "I just saw the best dog! She's a big old English mastiff, and she's so beautiful! The dog-rescue lady from next door brought her into the store today. She needs a permanent home. Can I take her?"

"Your dad won't be too happy," I said, thinking of our two cats, and the Great Dane named Onyx that Seleta had convinced me to adopt, supposedly as a birthday gift for her father.

"Please, Mom? At least come see her."

I went down to the pet store, and there I met Maya. "Isn't she beautiful, Mom?" Seleta said.

That thing? She was gigantic, almost as big as our Great Dane. Plus, she drooled. But when I looked away from the dog and back at my daughter, I saw she was beaming, in a way I hadn't seen in a long, long time. Well, Seleta does want to go away to school, I convinced myself. A dog would be a good companion, and one that big certainly would be protection for a young woman living on her own.

"Okay," I agreed. "But only if, when you go away to Denver, she goes along with you." We paid the thirty-dollar

149

adoption fee and took the dog to our vet, Phil Trokey; he'd been taking care of our pets for years. "Maya's in excellent health," he assured us after the exam. So we brought her home for good.

Seleta enrolled Maya in an obedience class, where she sailed through with flying colors. "She's better than all the other dogs, Mom," Seleta told me. "She does almost everything she's supposed to do when she's told to do it." Seleta would come home from class and show us the latest command Maya had learned to obey. She was so excited that for the first time in a long while, I allowed myself to feel a bit of hope. The same girl who once could barely drag herself out of bed was now doing something that made her feel good. I prayed it would last.

One day, in the waiting room at the vet's, a little boy came over to Maya and started petting her. She was very gentle, as always, and even seemed careful not to drool on the little fellow. Not that he would have minded. He was delighted with the giant dog. "I don't know why I didn't think of this before," Phil said. "Maya is good with people. You might want to look into her becoming a therapy dog."

A big smile appeared on Seleta's face as soon as Phil spoke those words. She found a trainer and started working to get Maya ready for the tests she'd need to pass to be certified as a therapy dog. Meanwhile, the summer I'd worried so much about was coming to a close. Seleta pulled through it just fine. When school started she managed to juggle schoolwork and the training classes with Maya.

Seleta called the behavioral health center where she'd been a patient, and asked if they'd be interested in a therapy dog.

She was told to bring Maya in for an interview. The staff loved the dog so much that they said they'd be glad to have her and Seleta come in twice a week after she got her certification. When she heard that, it was like she came back to life all at once.

Training Maya for therapy had become therapy in itself. Now when Seleta took Maya out for walks she would introduce the dog to anyone they came across. One day she went over to the grounds of the elementary school next to our house. A few of the teachers fell immediately in love with Maya. "You know," said one of them, "Maya looks just like Mudge."

"Who?"

"It's a dog in a children's book series. A boy named Henry gets a huge dog named Mudge, and they become the best of friends. My students love those books. Say," she went on, "why don't you come to my class with Maya one day and read one of the books to the class. They'd love it!"

Seleta went, and the kids did love it. Soon after that, we visited my grandmother, who lives in a nursing home. Maya came along to meet Seleta's great-grandmother and all the other residents of the home. One elderly woman who sat with a stuffed puppy in her arms took a real liking to Maya. Seleta spent a long time with the woman, and they both talked about their dogs. At the end of the visit, both the woman and my daughter looked happy. Already, even before getting her certification, Maya was a success at pet therapy.

I'm not saying that Seleta's depression just vanished overnight. But somehow, working with Maya made it easier for Seleta to cope. Eventually she got engaged with the world and with people again. Maya made her want to. And that helped her maintain a balance. I took it in stride when Seleta announced that she wanted to be a foster parent for other rescued mastiffs. But I was floored when we started doing some research. The average adoption fee for an abandoned mastiff was $350. It seemed a bit steep, especially since almost all those abandoned dogs were in poor shape, with severe health problems or some kind of disfigurement.

I thought of Maya. She had been in perfect health, and she was as gentle as a lamb. Why would someone have abandoned her? A mastiff puppy in good shape could cost as much as fifteen hundred dollars. There was no way we would have been able to afford that. Yet our adoption fee was a mere thirty dollars.

How and why had it all happened? Well, I know Maya's a dog, but to me she's also kind of an angel. She came as an answer to prayer, didn't she?

Maya got her certification as a therapy dog, and now when she and Seleta leave the house to head for the nursing home, I see how content my daughter is. She's doing work that means something, giving of herself to people in need.

Seleta's leaving for Denver this month. I used to worry what might happen to her away from home, but now I know she'll be okay. After all, she's taking Maya along, and already they've made arrangements to do pet therapy at a children's hospital there. I'm sure Maya will mean as much to those children as she does to our family. I thank God every day for the giant, drooling dog who has been my daughter's guide to life.

Our Guard(ian) Dog

Elizabeth Polk

My daddy, Joe Norton, was a traveling preacher. Back in the forties, when we didn't have a car, he rode buses all over, bringing the Word of God to towns that were too small and too poor to have their own preachers. The five of us—Daddy, Mama, my big brothers, John and Bobby, and me—lived in a tiny town ourselves, out by the oil fields of west Texas. Hamlin was the kind of place where folks didn't even have locks on their doors, they trusted each other so much. When Daddy had to be away for a week or two at a stretch, he could rest assured we were safe at home.

I couldn't, though. I had a hard time getting to sleep when he was gone. My brothers didn't help any. They kept right on telling me tales about who might be lurking in the attic and they kept teasing me mercilessly about my reddish-brown hair. Usually the boys had the bunk beds in the kitchen across from the back door. But Mama knew how anxious I got when Daddy wasn't around. She would put the boys in the bedroom, then give me the top bunk and take the bottom one herself, so I'd feel more secure. I'd climb into bed with my favorite doll, Trudy, whose expression changed when you turned her head. I made sure Trudy's sleeping face was showing, but then I would lie awake myself, my mind awhirl with all the scary things that might happen without Daddy around. "He says God always takes care of us, Trudy," I'd whisper to my doll. "Well, I sure do hope it's true."

The summer I was nine I hoped more fervently than ever, because something terrible happened—something no one in Hamlin could remember ever happening before—and we needed extra protection. A burglar was on the loose—a stranger going around breaking into houses, stealing things and hurting people who got in his way. What if the burglar came to our house while Daddy was gone? What if he got me?

Daddy didn't want to leave us. Still he had made a commitment to folks out of town and we knew he couldn't go back on his word. So one July day we went to the bus station to see him off. Daddy asked us kids to mind Mama, then we held hands and prayed. Just before he got on the bus, Daddy opened his Bible and gave us a short reading from Psalms, his voice more serious than a month of Sundays: "The angel of the Lord encampeth round them that fear him, and delivereth them."

I repeated that verse to myself as we shaded our eyes and watched the bus pull away. When it was just a speck in the distance, we turned and headed home. Mama was quiet, and I could tell by the crinkles in her forehead she was worried.

"Hey, Libby," Bobby said to me, "your hair looks like an exploded can of tomato soup!" With a whoop, he and John took off down the dirt road, their shoes kicking up clouds of dust behind them.

Suddenly I felt as lonely as the single oil pump standing in a field nearby, slowly bobbing its head. We passed our little white clapboard church, its lawn browned to a crisp by the sun, and I tried not to think about how much I already missed Daddy.

Coming up our walk, I heard Bobby holler, "Look at that dog!" I followed his pointing finger to our front porch, where a huge, mottled creature was sprawled at the top of the steps, taking an afternoon snooze. John whistled. "Never seen anything like him!"

None of us had. Hamlin was such a small town, we knew everyone, even the dogs, and this one was definitely a stranger to these parts.

Bobby threw a few pebbles in his direction. The dog lifted his massive head, half-perking one ear, and surveyed us lazily, as if we were on his porch.

Holding tight to Mama's hand, I approached the dog and warily started up the steps.

"He sure is ugly," John said.

"Go away, dog!" Mama commanded. "Scat!"

The dog didn't budge. He just stared at us with those black eyes that were as shiny as marbles. Sighing, Mama stepped over him, turned and lifted me across his bulk. John was right behind us. Bobby poked the dog with his foot before he jumped over him.

Creeeak. Mama opened the screen door. "Just leave him be," she said. "Soon as he figures out we can't feed him, he'll go away."

But he didn't. That night, after we said our prayers and went to bed, the dog occupied my mind even more than the burglar did. I wondered if he'd still be there when we woke up. Sure enough, he was. We tried to shoo him away, but he paid us no mind. When Bobby nudged him, the dog didn't so much as blink. That night I checked outside before I went to bed, and he was lying on the front porch in the same spot. He stayed there for several days straight. I never once saw him leave the porch.

Before we knew it, Mama was telling us, "Daddy's due back tomorrow." That evening the crinkles in Mama's forehead smoothed out, and she smiled a lot during dinner. One more night till Daddy came home. One more night till I didn't have to be scared of the burglar breaking into our house.

It got dark out, and Mama gathered us around the kitchen table to pray. We asked God to keep us all safe—Daddy on the road, and the four of us at home. Mama sent us off to bed with a reminder. "Remember the Psalm your daddy gave us," she said. "The angel of the Lord is looking out for us."

I climbed up the ladder into my bunk with my Trudy doll and turned her head so she was sleeping. Then I laid my own head on the pillow. Mama switched off the light and went to tell John and Bobby good night. When she came back, she flipped on the floor fan, pulled back the sheets and slid into the bottom bunk.

"'Night, Mama," I said, swinging my hand over the side of the bed.

Mama reached up and squeezed my hand. "'Night, Libby. Sleep tight."

The light from the alley behind our house shone into the room and hit the blades of the fan, making strange, shifting silhouettes on the wall. Sometimes I pretended they were people dancing at a fancy ball, but that night they looked more like a gang of burglars coming after me. I yanked the covers up so no one could see me. *Daddy, I wish you were here.*

Creeeak. What was that? It sounded like the screen door in back. I peeked over the edge of my covers. A looming shadow moved across the wall as the back door eased open.

"Mama!" I hissed, my heart thumping so loud I was sure the burglar could hear.

"Shh," she said. "I see him!"

I closed my eyes tight, not wanting to witness what the burglar would do to us. "God, help us, please!" I whispered, hugging Trudy against me.

At that moment, I heard a sharp bark. Then a low, menacing growl. Closer and closer it came. Suddenly it stopped.

I couldn't stand it anymore. I opened my eyes and turned toward the door. Mama leaped out of bed and grabbed a knife from the kitchen drawer. I cringed as she opened the door all the way.

Only there was no burglar out back. Just the dog. The extra-large, funny-looking, black-and-gold dog who had camped out on our front porch and refused to move for anything, except . . . Except he'd run all the way around back and leaped the fence to protect us from the intruder. Now the dog was sitting there at our back door, facing us calmly, as if nothing had happened.

Mama gave him a pat on the head and closed the door.

She put the knife away and got into bed. "The dog is keeping watch, Libby, so we're safe. Go to sleep."

I woke to the sun shining in my eyes. Daddy's coming home! I turned Trudy's head so she was smiling and climbed down the ladder. Mama's bed was already made. Hearing a noise from the front porch, I peeked outside. Mama was out there talking to the dog, who had returned to his usual spot. She'd given him a bowl of water and fixed some biscuits and gravy for him. I couldn't make out what she was saying, but I figured it must have been something along the lines of what I was thinking. *You're our angel, dog. Thank you.*

Three o'clock that afternoon we went to the bus station to meet Daddy. As soon as he stepped off the bus, I ran to him.

"Hi, girl!" Daddy said, whirling me around in his arms. "I missed you."

"I missed you too," I said. "You gotta see our new dog. He saved us from the burglar!"

All the way home, John and Bobby and I talked about the dog. How big and distinctive-looking he was. How brave. We couldn't wait for Daddy to see for himself. But when we came up to our house, the dog wasn't on the porch. He wasn't out back. He wasn't anywhere to be seen.

I thought the dog might turn up the next time Daddy went away, but he never visited our house again. I guess he didn't have to, because by that point I'd learned that even though Daddy couldn't be there every second to protect us, the God he preached about always was, standing guard with his angels, who come in all shapes and sizes and colors.

Brave Companion

Kathleen Fornataro

I t was the first warm day after winter, when the snow and cold have finally gone for good. After I got home from my job as a dental assistant, I threw open my windows, changed into sweats and did a little spring cleaning. As I vacuumed I was careful to maneuver around Ginger, my ancient Pomeranian, who was napping peacefully in a swath of sunlight. Age and complacency had probably made her oblivious to my racket; still, I didn't want to disturb her.

When I finished, I sat down in my recliner and flicked on the TV, waiting for my son, Tony, and my husband, Al, to get home from work. All at once I felt a swell of loneliness. My daughter had recently moved to an apartment, and Tony was rarely home except to sleep and catch an occasional bite to eat. Al was busier than ever at work, or always at his workshop out in the garage.

Oh, I knew Al loved me, though the longer we were married—nearly thirty years then—the less I seemed to see of him. Was I just feeling my age? Was this what they meant by "empty nest syndrome"?

Well, there was always Ginger, five pounds of utter devotion. She was toothless and deaf and hobbled around on

159

arthritic legs. Because of a heart condition she spent most of her time snoozing. But she still followed me from room to room. No, I would never be alone as long as Ginger was around.

I flipped through the TV channels until I found the news. They were giving the weather when I heard someone come through the front door, humming. Sounds like Tony's home, I thought.

A young man walked into the living room. He wore faded, frayed jeans and an oxford-cloth shirt with a T-shirt underneath. For an instant I thought he might be a friend of Tony's, yet there was no sign of my son. One look in the stranger's eyes and I knew that something was dreadfully wrong.

"You're all alike," he mumbled, fixing me with a glassy stare. "You're out to get me. Well, I'm not going to let you."

He loomed over me, jittery, mumbling and humming. I felt myself turn cold with fear inside. Clearly, he was deranged. There was no telling what he wanted.

Al, where are you? Come home! Right now!

I glanced over at Ginger. Still asleep. Then the man spoke again, but with a sharper, more menacing tone. "You want to hurt me! You won't get me! I'll hurt you first!"

His fists were clenched and perspiration trickled down his brow. *Please, Lord, don't let him hurt me. Don't let him hurt Ginger.* All at once he sat down on the couch, glowering at me, then announced. "Your husband's dead. I just killed him. Outside."

All the breath went out of me, as if I had been dealt a tremendous physical blow. *Al? Dead? Dear God . . .* Even as I tried to deny it, I had no doubt this man was capable of killing. I could see it in his eyes.

He was on his feet again, waving and ranting. I got up, gripping the back of the couch for support. I was no match for him, but I wasn't going to just sit there in my recliner while he murdered me. What made a person like this? Drugs? Mental illness? *God, be with me now, I prayed. You are my only hope.*

I was nearly face to face with him. I sensed his rage, like a blast of wind. He began to raise his hands. I set myself, too frightened to move yet determined to fight.

Out of the corner of my eye I saw something. A movement, a tiny blur of burnt orange. Ginger, no!

She barked furiously, charging stiff-legged across the living room directly at the intruder. There was no fear in her eyes, just fury and determination. Before the man could react, Ginger clamped her mouth on his leg, gumming at his ankle. I started to move.

One swift kick from him and she's finished. . . .

Taken by surprise, he shrieked. Thrashing and screaming, he jerked back his leg. But Ginger was relentless, growling and yipping. Finally he did kick her, like a rag doll, across the room, where she hit the wall with a thud and crashed to the floor, yelping in pain.

I stepped back. I really was ready to fight him. *You can't get away with this!* For the first time in my life, I wanted to hurt another human being. But when I looked into his eyes he seemed more frightened than angry. Ginger's attack had thrown him into confusion. He babbled distractedly as I dashed across the room and cuddled trembling Ginger to my chest. *Maybe we can slip away . . .*

We didn't have to. Staring wide-eyed at us, then backing off, the man turned and tore out the front door. Clutching Ginger in one arm, I picked up the phone and dialed 911. I stole a glance out the window and realized I wouldn't need to speak to the operator. Three police cars, lights flashing, were in front of the house. My attacker had been subdued and handcuffed, still ranting incoherently.

Al! I dropped the phone, ran out onto the porch and right into a policeman, who tried to calm me down and ease me back inside. "My husband, he's been . . . You've got to help him . . . " I heard myself gasping. Then I saw the single most beautiful sight in all the world: Al's truck turning sharply into our driveway. The horrible man had lied. Al was alive. He ran into the house, wondering what the excitement was about. He was quite shaken, but relieved I was okay.

We held each other as a police sergeant explained that the intruder was mentally ill and had been on a rampage after having discontinued his medication. "You were lucky," he said. "He attacked four people before he got here."

How could I tell the officer that luck had had nothing at all to do with it? That God had answered my desperate prayer by giving my wheezing, five-pound Pomeranian the strength and courage to rescue us from danger?

Ginger suffered no ill effects from the encounter, and

neither did I. In fact, I noticed my son staying home with me more often, and my daughter made it a point to drop by a couple of times a week. Al spent fewer hours in his workshop and more time with me, and my nest began to feel a little less empty.

Then there was Ginger, the bravest and most devoted companion I could hope for. Sometimes God chooses his smallest creatures to show his greatest love.

Ginny to
the Rescue!

Philip Gonzalez

Not all that many years ago I would have described myself as a happy, independent guy, proud of my work as a steamfitter in New York City—a job that paid well. I biked, sometimes twenty miles a day, played handball, and swam in the ocean near my place in Long Beach. At forty, I lived a bachelor's life to the fullest—no financial obligations beyond my apartment, vacations anywhere I wanted, and partying with friends every night.

My pals and I were tough guys, all of us. But there was one thing they used to razz me about—my weakness for animals. It went back to when I was a kid. I took in a stray kitten at age nine and later convinced my family to adopt an old dog whose owner had died. After I moved to Long Beach I'd saved an unwanted pup from being drowned, and found a home for an ex-girlfriend's cats. Once, on a building site in downtown Manhattan, I spotted a mother rat with a nest of babies, and I left food for her every day. "It's just a rat," my buddies said, but I thought of her as one of God's creatures who needed help.

I never figured I'd put myself in that category. Then, on the job one afternoon in January 1990, my heavy-denim engineer's coat got caught in a pipe-cutting machine. It chewed up my right arm, whirling me like a rag doll, pounding my head repeatedly on the concrete floor. I yelled until someone pulled the plug on the machine, and when it finally released me from its grip I was rushed to the hospital. The bones in my arm were crushed. I refused to let the doctors amputate, so they used microsurgery to save as many nerves as possible. Regular physical therapy might keep the arm from atrophying, but there were no guarantees. My hand would be practically useless, and I could eventually lose my arm.

Nearly two weeks later, wrapped in bandages and still groggy, I returned to my apartment. I sat around for days, not even changing clothes, because it was too hard. I didn't shave or get a haircut. What was the use? My buddies stopped coming by. I couldn't work, bike, play ball, or swim anymore. I only went out for my therapy appointments. I had to make do on a limited disability income. The best part of my life was over. So I just gave up, on myself and God.

My neighbor Sheilah was the only loyal friend I had. She often knocked on my door, trying to cheer me. One morning she invited herself in. "You've been hanging around this apartment for a month. We're going out." Too depressed to argue, I changed clothes and managed a lopsided shave. Sheilah grumbled about my ragged appearance as we got into her car. "Next stop, the animal shelter," she announced. "You're getting a dog."

"I can't take care of myself," I said. "How can I take care of a dog?" Sheilah just smiled, and by the time we hit the parking lot I'd changed my mind. A *big, male dog. German* shepherd, maybe. Purebred. A great-looking dog people will admire. Then they won't notice me.

The shelter attendant took one look at me, a bum with his arm in a sling, and immediately suggested a cat. "A nice, easy pet," he said.

"No, a big dog," I insisted, so he showed me a Doberman, a female. "I had a male in mind," I said.

As we started to move along I noticed a smaller dog curled into a corner of the Doberman's cage. A German shepherd puppy, maybe. I started to question the attendant when the pooch struggled to its feet. Definitely not a German shepherd. It was wirehaired and peculiar-looking, unlike any dog I'd ever seen. "That one's a female too, about a year old," the attendant said. The pup had been abandoned. "Isn't she cute?" asked Sheilah. The dog limped toward me. Her shoulders were broad, but her body was long and skinny, her legs thin and crooked. She had a bright-eyed face with white eyebrows and whiskers.

"She's not for me," I said. But the little dog was very friendly, begging for my attention, licking my fingers through the bars of the cage.

"That's the first time she's been on her feet since she got spayed," the attendant said. He suggested taking her outside for a walk. "She could use the exercise," he said.

"So could you, Phil," Sheilah added. "Go ahead."

What a pair we were: the dog with stitches in her belly, me with staples in my arm. Handling the leash with my left hand was almost as awkward as shaving with it. *Can't I walk a dog anymore, God? Can't I even do that?* We'd gone only a half block when the dog sat down and looked up at me. I felt a jolt of recognition when our eyes met, like a connection being made. "You're going home with me," I said. I could swear she smiled.

I named her Ginny. She adjusted to my apartment right away, and I decided to introduce her to the neighborhood that first afternoon. I worried she'd be too much for me, but Ginny hobbled along beside me without pulling on her leash, perfectly behaved, as if we were old friends.

We went walking the next morning, later in the afternoon, and several times the following day. It felt good to get outside again, and I found myself looking forward to our walks. On one of our strolls Ginny got excited when she saw a small yellow cat rummaging around a garbage can. My hand tightened on the leash, but Ginny pulled free. "Stop!" I yelled. Dogs hate cats. Ginny dashed for the cat and I feared the worst. But I watched in amazement as Ginny began licking the homeless creature as its mother would have done. The cat licked her in return and followed us home. Ginny wagged her tail when I shared some of her dog food with her new friend.

The next morning the cat was waiting outside our door with several others. Ginny pranced around them like a proud mama. A few tagged along when Ginny and I went for our walk. My neighbors waved when they saw our little parade.

"That dog loves cats," Sheilah said one day, watching Ginny cavort with her alley cat pals. "Why not get her a kitten of her own?" I frowned. Another pet? But when Ginny settled down and one of the cats curled up on her flank and fell asleep, I gave in.

Once again Sheilah and I drove to the animal shelter. Ginny came with us. At a cageful of kittens, she immediately headed for a white one, who began purring like a tiny outboard motor when Ginny started to groom her. I called the kitty Madame, and she joined our household.

Soon after, Ginny led me to a cat being abused by some neighborhood kids. We rescued her and took her home. After living on the streets she was hostile, cowering in a corner, hissing at us. Ginny patiently stayed close, giving her tongue baths when she finally ventured out of her corner. I named her Vogue, and Ginny got her to trust us, even to nap on my chest as Ginny lay by my side in the recliner.

Another time Ginny raced into an abandoned building and returned with a kitten in her mouth. The vet told us the kitten had a muscular defect and advised putting her down. We took her home, named her Topsy, and she thrived under Ginny's care.

I had adopted a dog, and she had adopted three cats. Ginny loved all cats, but she had a special affinity for those who were handicapped or lost. What I didn't realize was the change she was bringing about in me. Day by day I was getting stronger.

I slept in my recliner to keep my injured arm and hand elevated as the doctors had recommended. One night I was awakened at 1:00 A.M. Ginny was pacing excitedly in the room. Twisting around, trying to quiet her, I looked down at my right hand. I could have sworn that my fingers moved. Impossible! Even with all my physical therapy I hadn't been able to move my arm, and my hand had remained useless.

Ginny was circling the room, happily barking as if someone else were there with us. "What is it, girl?" My mother always said dogs could see angels. *If that's true*, I thought, laughing, *Ginny can see the angel who moved my fingers. Because that's about what it would take.* The cats were alert too, watching Ginny. I looked at my hand again. My fingers were definitely moving. The doctors had held out little hope of my regaining any use of them. Was I dreaming?

After a few minutes Ginny calmed down. The cats curled up and Ginny resumed her place beside me. We all fell back to sleep. The next morning I'd forgotten about my "dream." Then, when I was making coffee, my right hand moved. Just a little, but it moved.

At my physical therapist's later that day I excitedly told her about my hand. "Impossible," she said. "Watch this," I countered, and started moving my fingers. She brought a doctor in, and I moved my fingers again. "Maybe the nerves are starting to reattach themselves," the therapist said. They gave me a new brace and assigned special exercises to strengthen my fingers. Today I've regained some use of my hand, and my arm no longer hangs limp at my side.

Ginny continues being a kind of angel to needy cats, rescuing more than three hundred at last count. We have nine sharing our apartment, and scores more who show up on the doorstep for regular meals. I count myself as one of the strays Ginny found and nursed back to health—with help, perhaps, from an angel from heaven.

A Lifetime of

Laughter and Joy

Compact Gods

Elisabeth Rose

On the Christmas morning of my eleventh year, as I stood walking a new Slinky from hand to hand, my little sister shrieked "A puppy!" and a roly-poly wirehaired fox terrier pup came tumbling across the rug. My sister fell to her knees and scooped the puppy up, but I, stunned, dropped the Slinky and sank slowly to the couch. A dog. My dog. She was finally here. My *parents*, I told myself, *will never regret this. Never will either of them have to feed her, or walk her, or discipline her. Never will I give them any reason to say "I'm sorry we ever let you have that dog."* The responsibility kept me seated on that couch for a good long moment. In fact, it surprised everyone, even me, that I didn't rush to the dog as my sister had, but I was thinking, *We have the rest of our lives together.*

The rest of our lives together lasted only six years, but Patches and I filled those six. She played such a fine game of soccer—dashing left and right, kicking the ball with her front paws and retaining it with her chin—that in our neighborhood, soccer was a game of eleven kids against one terrier. I tied her leash to my three-speed bike, a Raleigh Chopper with a banana seat, and she pulled it while I did stunts, such as standing on the seat like a surfer. She loved to go sledding, so when it snowed I took her—Patches pulling the sled to the golf course where scores of people rode a rolling hill half a mile long. At the top, Patches sat on the sled alone, waiting for a push, and when I gave her a shove, I watched her sit there, the back of her head, shoulders, and black saddle patch going down, getting smaller and smaller, until at the bottom when the sled stopped, she jumped off wagging her stubby tail, and pulled the sled back up the hill herself.

Determined to keep my parents from regretting her, I took her to a 4-H obedience class and worked her several times a week despite the universal consensus that fox terriers are intractable boneheads. My parents had nicknamed her "El Stupido," "El Dumbo," and "Toad." Some of the more competitive kids in the 4-H class, like the girl who had a small, well-primped and puffy robot of a sheltie, wouldn't even look at us until we'd won obedience ribbons. Even the instructor shook her head at us a lot at first. Patches introduced herself by pooping right in the middle of the room. During her long down-stay, she rolled over, deliriously kicking her legs in the air and scratching her back. Although she made everyone smile by brazenly preferring life's gustier pleasures, no one listened when I insisted that, like any class clown, she wasn't stupid, just uncooperative. She was like most people I knew: she'd only work if you gave her a good reason to.

I gave her good reasons—a choke collar, treats, praise, play. Each summer at the 4-H dog show, she won obedience ribbons and trophies. The first summer, when we entered Tricks, she even upstaged me. I had taught her nine tricks, and we practiced them in the kitchen, in order, several times a day—such simple tricks as "shake," "other paw," "speak," "roll over," "be a ballerina" (stand on hind legs and twirl), and "jump" (jump over my raised leg). When the moment arrived, we strode to the center of the ring, the crowd silenced, I held up the treat, gave the first command, and Patches whipped through all nine tricks, without me. She lifted, shook, and lowered each paw; yapped; rolled in the sawdust; stood all the way up and twirled; sprang back and forth over nothing. The judge almost fell off her chair laughing, and the crowd, after a confused silence, burst into applause. When I failed to toss her a well-earned treat, Patches soloed the entire routine again while I stood beet red and nearly in tears, for she hadn't played right, had confirmed my fear that she didn't need me, had proved she didn't really obey. Of course, I was wrong, she had more than obeyed me. She had understood her role in the dog show, taken it on, and transcended it, performing much more than the puppetry I had planned.

That day, along with several other ribbons and a Best in Show trophy, we took home the blue ribbon in Tricks, overturning the sheltie throne.

A Glimmer of Intelligence

Margo Kaufman

Halfway down the corridor, I heard her whimper like Camille. Had I been home, I would have kept walking. Such is an advantage of home ownership. But I was in a hotel, dependent on the kindness of a tenderhearted owner who wouldn't be nearly so tenderhearted if another guest complained.

I unlocked the door. I stated the obvious. "You want to come."

Duh, thought Clara.

I unzipped her black bag.

Sucker, thought Clara. She gave me a patronizing smile, displaying two crooked jack-o'-lantern teeth, and scampered into the bag. She snuggled on her blanket and remained silent as I carried her through the lobby.

Mother's eyes narrowed as I climbed into the front seat. "Where did you get that purse?" she asked. "It's too big for you."

I partially unzipped the bag, and Clara's head popped out like a periscope. She peered at the leather bucket seats. She reasoned, *What am I doing, in this hot bag?* She climbed out and made a nest on the armrest.

174

"I don't think it's smart to bring her," said Mother.

"You're right," I agreed. "But she wants to come."

Clara flared her mushroom nostrils, fixed Mother in her crosshairs, and attempted to bend Mother's will—a task I've never managed in my lifetime. I watched with fascination as Clara willfully turned up the volume of her own cuteness. She extended her front paws and stretched languidly. Her lips parted ever so slightly to reveal a glimpse of rosebud-pink tongue. Her entire being became smaller and squarer.

Mother shrugged, started the car, and cut in front of a bus. "You were just like that when you were a little girl," she said. "I used to take you everywhere."

She miraculously found a parking space on the street a block from Saks. I said, "Clara, get in the bag," and, after a quick deliberation as to whether this action was in her own best interest, the pug made a dramatic leap. As we rode the escalator to the fifth floor, she peeped through the mesh ventilation panels at all the luckless shoppers who would never get a chance to stroke her glossy black coat. She sent a telepathic entreaty to Mother, who was rapidly settling into her role as doting grandmother.

"Clara is too warm," Mother said. She partially unzipped the bag, and the periscope emerged. Once we reached the Fifth Avenue Club, the plush lounge where customers who patronize the store's personal shoppers get to try on clothes, Mother declared that Clara preferred to sit on the comfy chintz couch.

I was not enthusiastic. I recalled the day that I picked

Sophie up from Paul Winfield. She was five months old. I'd brought along a portable Sky Kennel and carefully placed the puppy inside it so she wouldn't feel insecure on the long drive home. Duke had asked me to stop by his office with the new member of the family. I carried Sophie's box into his office and opened the kennel door. Sophie refused to come out.

"She's scared," Duke said in his gentlest voice. He whispered sweet nothings into her cage, but Sophie wouldn't budge. Now that I know Sophie, I realize it wasn't fear, just obstinacy.

Back at Saks, I expressed concern that Clara might experience similar stranger-anxiety.

"Don't be ridiculous," Mother said, and released the puppy like Elsa the lioness in *Born Free*. Clara admired herself in the three-way mirror, then gracefully arranged herself on a thousand-dollar Armani skirt that a previous customer had discarded in a corner of the dressing room. When the personal shopper appeared, wearing so much costume jewelry she clanked, Clara sashayed over to greet her and sat demurely on her shoe. She widened her Bette Davis eyes until the shopper got the message and picked her up. Clara licked off half a pound of Clinique foundation and shed at least five dozen black hairs, but the shopper didn't mind. Instead, she rounded up a half-dozen of her immaculately dressed colleagues. Clara worked the crowded dressing room like [a candidate] on the campaign trail, occasionally raking her needle claws on a pair of seventy-dollar Wolford stockings.

Mother had a revelation. "She doesn't behave like a

dog," she whispered. "I've had dogs all my life, and that isn't what she is. She's a little person walking on all fours."

Initially, I suspected that Mother was laying it on so thick because she believed that Clara was the closest thing to a grandchild she was likely to get from me. But the longer I spent with Clara, the more I realized what Mother had seen immediately: Clara had powers. Still, for fifteen years I'd prided myself on treating my pets like dogs, not people, and I didn't intend to make an exception.

"Clara, would you like a glass of water?" asked the shopper.

"No, thank you," I said. Water, an unhousebroken puppy, and ivory carpet were not a good mix.

"Bottled water would be lovely," Mother said imperiously. "Clara's a little parched." Frankly, I was surprised she didn't suggest we stop by Rumpelmayer's so Clara could have an egg cream.

As if on cue, Clara panted dramatically, her rosebud tongue unfurled to twice its original size. The personal shopper hastily fetched a cut-crystal goblet and a bottle of Evian. From the way Clara attacked it, you would have thought she had been stranded in the Sahara for a month with a leaky canteen.

"Poor dear was thirsty," the shopper said reproachfully. I disliked having my parenting skills questioned by a total stranger. "She had water before we left."

Mother lowered her voice. "She was born to act. Like Shirley Temple, who at age four was an international star."

Mother was born to be a stage mother. I was a washout, but with Clara, she finally had her opportunity. She glanced at her watch, realized we were—gasp!—only an hour early for our next appointment, at Barneys, and dragged the pug away from the admiring throngs. She whispered to Clara, "Always leave them wanting more." To avoid having the pug suffer from loneliness on the ride down the escalator, Mother handed me the Sherpa Bag while she cradled Clara in her arms. The sight of the tiny black puppy pressed against Mother's white mink attracted the eye of nearly every shopper in the store.

That escalator ride taught Clara a valuable lesson: A pug gets more attention at eye level. Henceforth she would refuse to stand on an escalator; she automatically assumes the paws-locked position and makes me hold her aloft. She did, however, master elevators and revolving doors.

I never did find a dress, but by morning's end, Clara was the toast of Barneys, Bloomingdale's, Henri Bendel, and Bergdorf Goodman. Mother suggested that we take her "someplace special" for lunch, but I passed. Though Jacqueline Susann wrote that poodles used to be regularly checked at "21," I didn't think my mother's favorite haunts, Le Cirque and the Friars Club, were pug-friendly, so I brought her back to the Hotel San Carlos.

By the time we got to the lobby, I suspected the puppy's entire inside was one big bladder. When Gabriel at the front desk refused to turn over my room key until he'd met Clara—or, as he called her, because he was Spanish, "Clarita"—she sat placidly on the reception counter and allowed herself to be stroked by the doorman, the bellboy, and several of our fellow guests. She waited until we were back in our room, then she trotted into the bathroom, squatted gracefully on the *New York Times*, and returned to her command post on the sofa. She looked up at me eagerly as if to ask, *So, where are we going next?*

I wound up taking her to all my meetings, and she did my career a world of good. Normally, when I'm in New York I call on various publications to solicit assignments. Editors aren't thrilled to see a freelance writer, and before Clara, my average meeting lasted at most twenty minutes. But when I entered a magazine office with the world's most ingratiating puppy riding shotgun in my shoulder bag, the dynamic improved considerably. By the second meeting, Clara had worked out a fail-safe sales pitch. I gave my name to the gatekeeper, and ever so subtly the periscope rose from the bag and surveyed the situation. If she wasn't noticed immediately, she sneezed delicately or snorted. "What on earth do you have in that bag?" the gatekeeper would ask, and the pug would give her a conspiratorial wink, as if to say, *How clever of you to notice.*

Invariably, she'd be invited to come out of her bag. She emerged slowly, like Gypsy Rose Lee fingering a glove. She wobbled a little, like a newborn colt, to elicit sympathy, then made a beeline for the most powerful person in the room. I felt like Shari Lewis with Lamb Chop. Instead of promoting myself as a writer, I found myself providing color commentary for Clara's performance. "Yes, black pugs are rare." "No, she doesn't have breathing problems." "Yes, the Duke and Duchess of Windsor kept pugs too." In fact, they were bathed every day in Miss Dior perfume. Clara shares the Duke's birthday, but she's not proud of it.

I couldn't complain, even though Clara came away from these encounters with all sorts of souvenirs: bottled water, string cheese, squeak toys, a traveling feeding dish, even half a pastrami on rye, at places that didn't even offer me a Diet Coke. (This is the biggest difference between doing business on the East and West coasts. On the latter you are always served refreshments, even if you're about to be fired.) I was beholdened to Clara for her professional support. It was impossible for a snooty women's magazine editor to intimidate me or price my clothes when she was crawling on the floor with the pug. When I smuggled Clara into the *New York Times,* an editor at the Travel section insisted on carrying her over to meet an editor at the magazine who had heretofore failed to respond to any of my letters or calls. Clara was given a couple of copies of the paper (she favored the Home section) as a parting gift. I even got an assignment.

Her greatest triumph came at my publisher's office. My first book was about to come out, and I had gone to New York to meet my then-editor, David. He is not a pug person and seemed taken aback when exclamations of "Isn't she cute?" began ringing down the hall. (Then again, the man who was David's boss, publishing lord S. I. Newhouse, had a pug named Nero who every year was given a birthday party—complete with caviar and twenty pug guests—by the writer Alexandra Penney. Nero died, but his successor, Cicero, is similarly feted.) A sales meeting was in progress, and Clara was passed around the conference table with great reverence, like she was the author of the megaseller *Midnight in the Garden of Good and Evil*. She even got to meet Peter Gethers, whose famous cat, Norton, travels in a similar Sherpa Bag. "We may have to send Clara on tour with you," David said, and the buoyant pug kissed his nose, much to his chagrin.

By the end of her first visit to Manhattan, Clara had gotten me more assignments than my agent. "She's in control," said Loretta, who would later express regret that she had failed to sign Clara as a client at this time. "She's the cutest puppy in the world, and she has an attitude."

Mother drove us to the airport and made me promise to bring Clara back to New York at Christmastime so the pug could see the tree at Rockefeller Center. I was surprised she didn't offer to take her skating.

Our flight home was uneventful. Clara stayed in her bag, stowed under the seat in front of me, until the pilot turned off the Fasten Seat Belt sign. Then she mewed imploringly to be let out. I explained that it was against airline regulations. She assured me that she understood the need for stealth. (Clara would prove to be an accomplished sneak.) She snored quietly in my lap, hidden under a blanket, and only made her presence known when the stewardess came around with lunch. Clara awoke instantly and fired up her begging program. She put her paws on the armrest and stared at the meal cart. She savored the aroma of the prefabricated food. She licked her lips hopefully. (She may have been the first passenger in years to express eagerness for an airline meal.)

"Would Clara like a little steak?" the flight attendant asked. *Actually, Clara would.* She also ate my roll and half my fruit plate, and she drank water from a plastic cup. Somewhere over Denver I stuffed her back into her bag and carried her into the bathroom. I set the Home section of the *New York Times* on the floor, and she did her business. I was walking back to my seat when the stewardess asked, "Would Clara like to meet the pilot?" *Actually, Clara would,* and she returned from the cockpit with a set of American Airlines wings.

"At least they didn't let her fly the plane," Duke later said.

The stewardess allowed Clara to remain in my lap until we approached Los Angeles. Then she apologetically asked me to put her under the seat for landing. Clara darted into her bag without a protest.

Having conquered the sky, Mother, the publishing industry, and me, Clara felt pretty cocky when we landed at Los Angeles International Airport. Duke met us at the gate, took one look at her, and exclaimed, "She's the cutest thing I've ever seen." That was when I realized our future roles were cast: I'd be playing Margo Channing to Clara's Eve Harrington.

Only one hurdle remained.

How was Eve going to deal with Sophie?

Cleo for Short

Brooks Atkinson

S he was not an accomplished dog. No tricks, no spectacular rescues, no brilliant achievements—nothing to confound incredulous men. But she was a beautiful and loyal German shepherd dog, and she was infectiously happy. In the course of time she came to be a vital part of our family life. Now that she is gone, our home seems partly desolated. The corners in which she used to doze, smudging the baseboards, look gray and empty; the streets and waste lots where she used to frisk in the morning look dull. When we go to the country the fields seem deserted without her, for the places she most enjoyed took on some of the radiance of her personality and reflected her eagerness and good will.

Since dogs are relatively unimportant in the adult world, it is probably foolish to grieve when they go. But most people do grieve, inconsolably, for a time, and feel restless, lonely, and poor. An epoch in our lives was finished when Cleo (short for Cleopatra) died. Our relationship to the world was perceptibly altered. Nothing else can give us her exultant response to the common affairs of the day. Nothing can quite replace the happy good nature that was always greeting us when we came home or that was mischievously waking us up in the morning, hurrying us out-of-doors after breakfast, or innocently urging us to go to the country where we all wanted to be.

The place she made for herself in our world was of her own doing. I had no active part in it, particularly in the beginning. Although I am guilty of grieving now, I was innocent of hospitality in her first days among us. One Sunday morning in June when we were living on the farm, my brother called on the telephone. "How would you like to have a puppy?" he casually inquired. "Fine," I said with the heartiness of a man who had never had a dog but was willing to experiment. As an afterthought, "What kind?" I asked. "A police pup," he replied. "She's a stray dog. Been here a week. We don't know what to do with her." "Bring her along," I said, since I was already committed. After all, there could be no harm in a puppy.

About two hours later he drove into the dooryard. A huge, wild animal bounded out of the car and jumped up on me before I could recover my breath. A puppy? Goodness, she was alarming! Someone put a pan of water down for her. She lashed into it like a tiger. Someone opened a can of beef. She took the whole canful in two gulps, looking a little hungrily at the arm that fed her. To me, she looked savage and as she ran helter-skelter around the farm all afternoon—about seventy pounds of lightning. I was depressed. "I don't know about this animal," I said mournfully. "After all, I'm no lion tamer."

After her harrowing experience of being a lost dog, Cleo had taken in the situation at a glance, and was eager to settle down in a country household. Our first struggle came at bedtime. Like any other civilized man, I scorned dog-ridden homes, and I proposed to tie her on the porch at night until I could build her a doghouse. But that was far from being her idea of the way things were to be. Even while I was tying her, half expecting her to bite me or take me by the throat, she cried with more pathos than I liked, and she bellowed like a heartbroken baby when I put out the lights and went upstairs. Well, a man can't be mean indefinitely. After a miserable quarter of an hour I shuffled downstairs in my slippers to release her, as no doubt she knew I would. As soon as she was free she shot into the house, raced upstairs, and leaped on my bed. That settled our relationship permanently, about twelve hours after we had met. In time I was able to persuade her to sleep in the armchair near my bed or in a bed of her own, but no one ever again proposed to exclude her from any of the privileges of the family.

Since we live in New York most of the year, there was, of course, one other preliminary crisis. We had seen it coming and dreaded it, and no doubt she, too, knew something was in the air. We had intended boarding her with friends and neighbors for the winter: they liked her and would have taken good care of her in the broad country where any sensible dog would want to be. But when at length we started to pack the car one morning to go back to the city, Cleo flew into the back seat and stubbornly stayed there—partly in panic, partly in determination. She could not be expelled without more of a tussle than I had the will to provide. By this time I was more than half on her side. "Let's try her for a few days," I said with some misgivings, and our unwieldy caravan started to roll. Cleo liked the ride home. Cleo liked our apartment; she expanded as soon as she set four feet inside. She was so big and active that she appeared to occupy the whole of it. All evening she was delighted, and before we got up the next morning we heard her scampering and rushing around the living room with the clatter of a happy horse. When we finally emerged from the bedroom the sight was fairly dismaying. She had torn the stuffing out of an upholstered footstool and torn the pages out of a novel that had been affectionately inscribed by the author. But she raised no objections to a little explanatory discipline, and during the rest of her life she never destroyed property again. Although apartment living was confining, she clearly preferred to be with us in any circumstances, and, enormous though she was, she settled down to a city existence like a lady.

Make no mistake about it: the association was intimate. Cleo curled up on her own bed or slyly creeping up on mine on cold nights; Cleo under the breakfast table; Cleo under the writing table when I was working, jiggling my elbow when she concluded I had worked long enough; Cleo impatiently batting the Sunday newspaper out of my hands when I had been reading too long at a stretch; Cleo affectionately greeting the maid in the morning, barking at all the tradesmen, teasing my son or brother to take her to walk at inconvenient moments, going wild with excitement when I picked up the bag that we always took to the country—she absorbed, approved, and elaborated on every aspect of family life.

"Like man, like dog," was her motto. Her determination not to be discriminated against amounted to an obsession. She insisted on being in the bedroom when we slept and in the dining room when we ate. If we went swimming, so did she, ruining peaceful enjoyment. If we shut her in the next room when friends dropped in for the evening, she threw herself impatiently against the door until, for the sake of quiet, we released her. Fair enough—that was all she wanted. After politely greeting every guest in turn she would then lie quietly in a corner. "You're a pest," I used to say, generally patting her at the same time. "Go and read a good book," my wife would say with vexation. "What this dog needs is discipline," my mother used to say with tolerant disapproval. To be candid about it, the discipline was easy. Excepting for the essentials, there was none. Cleo could be trusted to do nothing treacherous or mean.

If she had had no personal charm, this close physical association would have been more annoying than endearing. But she was beautiful. Her head, which came up to my waist, was long and finely tapered. Her eyes were bright. Her ears were sharply pointed. By holding them proudly erect or letting them droop to one side she indicated whether she was eager or coquettish. In her best days she had a handsome coat and a patrician ruff at the neck. She stood well and held her tail primly. Her vanity was one of the most disarming things about her. Praise her mawkishly and she fairly melted with gratitude. She was an insufferable poseur. When I came home from work late at night and lounged for a few moments before going to bed, she would sit up erect on the couch, throw out her chest grandly, and draw her breath in short gasps to attract attention. When everyone in the room was praising her—although with tongue in cheek—she would alternate the profile with the full face to display all her glory. "The duchess," we used to call her when she was posing regally in the back seat of the open car. But she was no fool. She knew just how much irony we were mixing with the praise and she did not like to be laughed at. If she felt that the laughter was against her, she would crowd herself into a corner some distance away and stare at us with polite disapproval.

Not that my regard for her was based exclusively on her beauty and amusing personality. She had more than that to contribute; she had a positive value in the sphere of human relations. As soon as she came to the city the orbit of my life widened enormously and my acquaintance also broadened. To give Cleo the proper exercise and a little fun, it was necessary to find a place where she could run loose for an hour. That is how we came to frequent the open piers along the Hudson River. Before she joined our household I had often walked there with a kind of detached enjoyment of a pungent neighborhood. No one ever so much as acknowledged my existence on the piers. But with a big, affable dog as companion, I began to acquire prestige. It was astonishing; it was even exciting. Truck drivers liked to discuss her. Some of the longshoremen warmed up. Policemen took her seriously. The crews of the tugboats took a particular fancy to her. In the course of time they came to expect us around noon, and some of them saved bones and pieces of meat for her refreshment. She was all too eager to jump aboard and trot into the galley, and that delighted them. Eventually Cleo must have had fifty friends along the waterfront, and I had five or six. It was through Cleo that I came to meet Charley, who is one of my best friends, and is always ready for a crack of conversation in the warm office where he dispatches tugboats and distributes the gossip of the river.

On Saturdays and Sundays we explored deeper territory down to the Battery and around South Street, where barges tie up for the winter, or across the river to Hoboken, where ocean vessels dock. When Cleo trotted ahead as a sign of friendly intentions, I discovered that even in these distant quarters I, too, was cordially received, and we had great times together. On weekends we were thus in close touch with important affairs. Hardly a ship could dock or sail without our assistance. Sometimes when we were off our regular beat a tugboat we knew would toot us a greeting as she steamed by. "Hello, Cleo," the skipper would bellow pleasantly from the wheelhouse. A man, as well as a dog, could hold up his head on an occasion like that. Thus Cleo opened up a new life for me, and it was vastly enjoyable for both of us.

There is no moral to be drawn from this tale of Cleo. Although the misanthrope says that the more he sees of man the better he likes dogs, the circumstances are unequal. If Cleo never did a mean thing in her life, there was no reason why she should. Her requirements in life were simple and continuously fulfilled. She was as secure as any dog could be. But men live insecure lives; food and shelter are necessities they work for with considerable anxiety. In a complicated existence, which cannot be wholly understood, they have to use not only their instincts but their minds, and make frequent decisions. They have to acquire knowledge by persistent industry. Their family associations are not casual, but based on standards of permanence that result in an elaborate system of responsibilities. It takes varying degrees of heroism to meet all these problems squarely and live a noble life. Living a life honorably in an adult world is not a passive but a creative job.

For Cleo it was much simpler. As far as I could see, there was nothing creative about it. The food was good; it appeared in the kitchen on time. The house was warm, dry, and comfortable. Her winter and summer clothes came without effort. Her associations were agreeable, including three dogs—all male—of whom she was especially fond. It was easy to maintain a sunny disposition in circumstances like that. But it would be unfair to deny Cleo her personal sweetness and patience. Whether her life was simple or not, she did represent a standard of good conduct. Her instincts were fine. She was loyal and forgiving. She loved everyone in the home. Beyond that, she was joyous and beautiful and a constant symbol of happiness. Although she obviously emulated us, sometimes I wonder. Shouldn't I have emulated her?

The Dogs of My Life

Jan Fook

I am going to come straight to the point.

People are all very well in their own way, but they are not dogs. Therefore I will write of dogs.

This is a somewhat abbreviated version of the beginning of a favourite book of mine, written by "Elizabeth" and entitled *All the Dogs of My Life*. Dogs, she says, are free from the fluctuations of human relationships. "Once dogs love," she claims, "they love steadfastly, unchangingly, till their last breath. That is how I like to be loved. Therefore I shall write of dogs."

I do not really know why I write of dogs, but I do know that I love and have loved each of my dogs—not perhaps steadily, or unchangingly, but certainly till their last breath. And in my dogs, I perhaps see the story of my own life, with its fluctuations, its unsteadiness and changes, its losses, and its lessons. Therefore I will write of all the dogs of my life.

Frisky was a literal answer to prayer. I was raised in a seriously religious, churchgoing family. We were taught to eschew many of the material comforts of life, but somehow I couldn't forgo the idea of a dog. By age seven, I had been praying for a

191

dog for some years. Frisky, a black, white-star-chested kelpie, turned up, from out of nowhere, on the doorstep of our Sydney home, a 1950s suburban brick veneer. It was a dark and stormy night. It was almost as if God had sent her in a flash of lightning, a shivering mutt to warm the life of a too earnest child. My father, who could never quite manage to cloak his innate kindness, dug some well-chewed (by us) bones from the garbage for her to eat, and cleared a place in the overflowing garage for her to sleep. I remember marvelling at this rare glimpse of his generosity. He even decided to leave the garage door slightly ajar, risking valued security, so she could relieve herself during the night.

In some ways Frisky became an important symbol for my own secretly guarded independence, in a household with too little privacy of thought or action. She lasted a good sixteen years. She died the same year Elvis died, which was also the final year of my social-work study. My friends from this time understood my love for dogs. One in particular, Penny, did something about it. She bought me Peanuts, the gawky, gangly Old English sheepdog-cross, who looked like an Afghan Hound. Peanuts's life spanned the fraught period of my young adulthood. She came with me to set up home in a neighbouring city, Newcastle, where I had been driven further afield in the quest for employment. During her thirteen-year life with me, she inhabited nine different properties, in four different cities. She uprooted with us, as we struggled to find a career footing in the academy, in times not so conducive to the employment of younger people. Peanuts was not the ideal dog for this period of my life, but in some ways I grieved most for her. Her patience and affection I had often taken for granted in a life which was largely uncertain, sliding sporadically between dreams and disappointments. She represented all that was constant about those years, a reminder that home life could always be depended upon, even if career could not.

Although her life might have been generally unfulfilled, Peanuts had one spot of unadulterated joy. This was Chelsea, who to this day I also remember as my unadulterated joy. She came to us in a period of sacrifice and experiment, when my partner, Al, and I disrupted our cozy home life so he could take up employment in a town six hours away. The joy of Chelsea ended more than twenty years ago, yet the vision of her feisty face and ebony eyes is as clear to me now, as the fine fur of my beloved Minty who lies beside me as I write these words. The young wirehaired fox terrier pup Chelsea was one of those souls who was born already knowing its own place and its own value. Peanuts, Al, and I were smitten from the earliest moment. It was lucky she died young. I can only tell you that I cannot imagine the grief that the loss of a full dog-life of attachment to Chelsea would have brought. Nor do I want to imagine it. The day after she was run over, a good friend of ours phoned with the news he had won $142,000 in the lottery. I would have given back a million lottery prizes then, and today, if I could have had my bright girl back.

Peanuts and Chelsea both taught me about different kinds of loss, one about the grief of the slow and inevitable passing of life, and the other about the wrenching anguish when life is ripped out of your hands and heart. So with Zoe, I thought I would learn how to manage grief. I set out to find a replacement for Chelsea who was not really a replacement. She was to be like her, yet not. Accordingly I chose the runt of the first wirehaired fox terrier litter I could locate. She was small, dainty and doelike, where Chelsea had been robust, rambunctious and devilish. Zoe turned out to be the biggest mistake of my dog life. Smelly, antisocial, and hard of hearing, Zoe seemed only to use her considerable brainpower when scheming how to avoid toileting herself on command. Her speciality was soiling the house immediately after she had been taken outside for this very purpose. Once she managed to soil every room in our five-bedroom Edwardian country home, in one evening. It was as if she couldn't decide exactly which spot would be the most exasperating so was hedging her bets! Zoe was the oddest little dog character I have ever known, yet when she died, I think I learned more about attachment than any of my other more attractive dog family members had ever taught me. I understood then, I thought, something of the paradox of human existence, how the most fraught of relationships can still inspire love and care. She caused me much angst, but she was mine, for better or worse.

Bob was intended to be a radical departure from the trials and tribulations of Zoe. He was a male dog—our first ever. In many ways Bob was a victim of his gender. He began life as sweet-tempered as you could imagine, a dog of children's storybooks and fairy tales. He was also as handsome a wirehaired fox terrier as you could imagine. Straight of leg, direct of eye, he brought to mind an artist's model. Many pictures of wire-haired fox terriers I have seen look exactly like my Bob. But over the years, despite his looks, his hormones ruined him. He evolved into a bad-tempered, highly strung, handsome monster, with separation anxiety. He developed the ability to climb rose bushes (Cecile Brunner) in order to follow his loved ones over the fence and to work. It was about this point in time we hatched the completely inspired plan of acquiring a companion for Bob, a submissive girl dog who would not challenge his authority but would ease the anxiety of his day-time loneliness. So Nellie sneaked onto the scene.

The story of Nellie is the fairy story of gender relations gone right. Submissive and companionable she was. Non-challenging she also was. But somehow, within about two weeks, Nellie became top dog, although I don't think Bob was aware of this, even on the day of his death, six years later, from colon cancer. The neat little sheltie–scottie cross had the streetwise brains I have always wished I had been born with. I think it is true to say that with Nellie, both Al and I experienced what dog companionship was always made out to be in the books. My first major trip overseas to Europe, at the ripe age of thirty-seven, was marred only by my mind's constant image of her pointed little mouse face, her clear amber eyes scanning for direct contact with my soul. I had to seek regular "dog contact" overseas, in order to stave off feelings of home-sickness. Now, whenever one of us leaves on a too frequent trip, the dreaded suitcase in hand, little Nellie hangs back, the anticipated pain of "goodbye, be a good girl" overcoming her staunch temperament. Her loyalty inspires the same. She is a major reason I do not want to leave the house during the day and cut dinner engagements short at night.

The other major reason for this newfound delight in domesticity is Minty, the purebred Shetland sheepdog who has adopted me as his shepherd. The delicate yet stately creature has the looks of a prince and the soul of a baby. He is never much more than a metre from my side. If I inadvertently shut him out of the bathroom when I am inside, he will lie right outside the door, his little black hairs poking underneath to reassure me of his presence. His gentle being calms and sustains me. The way he runs to me and presses into my body, or sits quivering on my feet at the least frightening sound, kindles in me the most satisfying protective instincts. There is a huge responsibility inherent in being adopted by a trusting animal. It is a responsibility which I hope brings out a better side of me. Minty in my life has brought a warm contentedness, a delight and comfort in things small and ordinary. At the same time, he frees me up to be me. He has given me new vistas, opened up possibilities of new creative pursuits, of living with, and writing about, more dogs.

Maybe it is with Nellie and Minty that the dogs of my life will become my life.

Clara, the Hero?

Margo Kaufman

I never made a conscious decision to take Clara along on my first book tour; perhaps she made the arrangements and cut me out of the loop. When the publisher sent me a plane ticket to New York, a pet ticket for Clara was enclosed, and it hardly seemed in my best interest to refuse. The pug was a proven crowd pleaser, and I was at the bottom of the celebrity food chain. "It's a shame you aren't a victim of some kind," the publicist for the book had said wistfully. "I could have booked you on all the talk shows."

Like Evita off to Buenos Aires, Clara eagerly hopped into her Sherpa Bag without a backward glance at Sophie, who was staying behind with Duke. He dropped us off at the airport and tenderly bade farewell to the love of his life. She gave his nose a gentle lick before ducking her head into the bag so he could close her zipper. "Write if you get work," Duke told her. He dragged my big suitcases over to the curbside check-in and gave me a quick hug. "Take care of Sugarplum," he called out as he drove away.

Clara contentedly rode through the terminal on my left shoulder; my PowerBook was slung on my right. I had a few anxious moments when I went through security, as I had to perform a complicated maneuver: Unpack the PowerBook, pass it to a security guard. Unpack Clara, put her bag on the conveyor to be scanned, carry her through the metal detector. Act confident when her bone-shaped silver-plated ID tag sets off the metal detector and the pug has to be scanned again with that metal-detecting rod. Hand pug to security guard. Boot up computer to prove it isn't a bomb. Shut computer down, put it back in the case. Pry pug away from the fawning crowd of passengers and guards who are passing her around like the wonder ball. Stuff her back in the bag. Throw PowerBook and pug over my shoulder and, feeling like a pack mule, trudge half a mile to the gate.

Within a year, I performed this procedure so many times I could do it in my sleep. This first time, though, I made a critical mistake. I left Clara's bag partially unzipped so she could poke her head out. I set the bag on the floor while I waited in line at the gate. The passenger behind me tapped me on the shoulder. "Excuse me," he said, "but is that your dog over there?" Sure enough, Clara had escaped and was introducing herself to a flight attendant who was savoring a dish of vanilla yogurt. When I tried to remove the piggish puppy from the food source, she looked stricken. "Poor thing was hungry," the flight attendant said accusingly.

Frankly, a little hunger is not such a bad thing when you're taking a dog on a five-hour flight. But luck was with Clara: her new best friend was working our plane. The flight attendant allowed the pug to sit on the empty seat beside me and even brought her a disgusting-looking chickenlike product, which Clara accepted gratefully, even though she had already helped herself to half of my fruit plate. We landed at Kennedy Airport at eleven at night. It was freezing; Clara shivered pathetically. I stuffed her into the pink-and-green-striped sweater that makes her look like a bumblebee and pulled on my molting fifty-year-old mink coat. Blessedly, my mother had sent Willy, my stepfather Paul's driver, to pick us up. "Clarita, it's so good to see you," he exclaimed when she jumped into the back seat of the Town Car. And then, as an afterthought, "Hi, Margo."

On our way to Manhattan, I asked a favor that in all his years as a driver he had yet to hear. "Is there any grass between here and the city?" He looked stunned—only later did it occur to me that he probably thought I was asking for drugs—and I hastily explained that Clara would only go on lawn, ivy, or, in a pinch, weeds.

Willy miraculously located a patch of green in Queens. "It's cold out," he warned.

"Don't worry, she'll be quick," I said. I dragged her out of the warm Town Car, said, "Hurry up," and Clara obeyed instantly, much to Willy's surprise. He reported this to my mother.

"I can't believe you say, 'Hurry up,' and she goes to the bathroom," Mother marveled later. "Who told you that dog was brilliant?"

Again we were staying at the Hotel San Carlos, where Clara and I had first met. "Clarita, welcome back," cried Gabriel at the front desk. He admired her sweater and carried her behind the desk into the back room to introduce her to a few new employees. As an afterthought, "Credit card, Margo."

It didn't take me long to realize that my book tour was not going to be the ego-boosting experience that I had fantasized about. When you're sitting alone in a room with your word processor you can imagine yourself to be creating a literary sensation, but once it gets published, you realize that what you actually have produced is a product, much like cereal, and I was not Cheerios but rather a quirky brand of granola. Fortunately, I had taken the precaution of buying a baseball cap for Clara embroidered with the name of my book. Mother chauffeured us from bookstore to bookstore, where I signed my books so they couldn't be shipped back to the supplier and Clara drew worshipful crowds. Not the lines around the block that Colin Powell and Howard Stern brought out, but more people than I could have summoned on the strength of my own reputation. Clara made an exception to her only-work-for-food policy: she sat, lay down, shook hands, danced, and for the finale, she barked. Everyone was mesmerized. She even convinced the cynical bookstore managers to move my book from the dingy corner of the humor section to a prominent place in the window.

"I can't get over she doesn't mind wearing the hat," Mother said. "And she is such an agreeable little person. I told her that we had to take a walk because her mom was signing books, and she said, 'Okay, that's fine.'"

Clara took a limousine ride out to Connecticut, where I was booked on a local talk show. She sat in the seat opposite me the entire trip. Later, when I took her for a walk along Park Avenue to see a display of sculptures by the artist Fernando Botero, she was photographed next to a rotund bronze bird by a television news crew. A publicist at Random House even managed to plant the following item about her in William Norwich's column in the *New York Post*:

From Clara's Scrapbook
William Norwich, *New York Post*
Friday, March 19, 1993

What else? Just that ever since the *New York Times* declared the pug the society dog of the year, you see them everywhere. The latest sighting was an eight-month-old pug named Clara who flew recently to New York from Venice, California, with her owner, Random House author Margo Kaufman.

Margo came to town to promote her new book, *1-800-AM-I-NUTS?*, a collection of screwball stories about life in screwball Southern California. The good pug Clara, sporting a neon-pink visor that said "1-800-AM-I-NUTS?" and a pair of lime-green sunglasses, was dragged from city bookstore to city bookstore by Ms. Kaufman.

The only hitch was a detour at Tiffany's, the Fifth Avenue jewelers, where Clara got herself caught in the revolving door.

Hardly the breakfast little Clara intended, more about bones than baubles, and surely a sign that a certain royalty check must have been burning a hole in Ms. Kaufman's pocket.

Clara made her radio debut on the *Joan Hamburg Show*. The show's publicist was initially apprehensive about letting her in the studio. But the pug wouldn't dream of soiling the carpet; she was more interested in finding out whether a thoughtful sponsor had sent over a pizza that the host might like to share. When none materialized, Clara took a fast train to Lullabye Land. Her jolly snoring could be heard over the airwaves, but the host was tickled. She told her audience that Clara was the best-behaved puppy she'd ever seen. Clara walked out of the studio unimpressed. Perhaps she sensed that radio was not her forte; TV was her preferred medium. (A few weeks later in Portland, Oregon, she made an electrifying television debut, growling at a close-up of herself on the monitor and chironed with the caption "Clara.") Or perhaps she was saving her strength for the most impressive trick she has ever performed: Escape from New York.

We were scheduled to leave on Saturday, but on Thursday the weather reports were unanimously predicting a weekend of snow. I decided it would be wise to fly back Friday morning, but Mother vetoed my decision. "You can't go," she said. "I've made reservations at the Friars Club for dinner."

"I don't want to get trapped in a blizzard," I said.

"I made reservations," Mother said, and it was futile to argue.

When I awoke at five o'clock on Saturday morning, snow (a substance I hadn't seen in twenty years and hadn't missed) was falling. I took Clara outside, and though she flinched, she gingerly walked over the ice to her favorite patch of ivy at Fiftieth and Second and squatted. Our flight was scheduled to leave at nine, and the storm wasn't supposed to get bad until afternoon. I called American Airlines to confirm a second time. I was put on hold for forty minutes, serenaded with the haunting refrain of "Something Special in the Air." They certainly weren't special on the phone—I never did get through to a human; but eventually I was connected to the automatic flight-information menu, and a computer voice assured me that our flight was leaving on time.

The snow got heavier the closer the cab got to the airport. "Nothing is taking off in this," the cabby said, but at the terminal the curbside skycap was also confident the plane was leaving. I checked my bags. That left me with Clara and the PowerBook, each of which weighed eight pounds but soon felt more like twenty. I did the security juggling act and trekked about a mile to the gate. We even boarded on time.

Just as I was congratulating myself on getting out of New York under the wire, the captain came on and announced a half-hour wait for deicing (a word I usually associate with death). Out the window, I could see swirling snow and the shivering ground crew, looking like they'd just run the Iditerod. An hour passed. The captain announced another deicing delay. Another hour passed. The captain announced that the long runway was covered with snow, a fact I could see for myself. Ten minutes later, he delivered the *coup de grâce*—the airport was closed. I wasn't surprised.

However, I was flabbergasted when I inquired as to what the airline planned to do to assist me and the hundreds of other stranded travelers and the stewardess uttered the consoling words, "You're on your own." In the case of snow—an act of God—the airlines aren't required to be helpful. I asked a customer-service representative at the gate to give me back my ticket. "Nobody else asked for that," she said brusquely. (This has become the stock response to any request for service in the nineties.) I insisted and eventually, after a stampede by other passengers, she relented. "What are we supposed to do?" I inquired.

"Go home," the customer-service representative said. As if that wasn't precisely the service I was depending on the airline to provide. "Call our 800 number for reservations."

If I had called that 800 number, I'd probably still be on hold. Instead, I went to the ticket counter. A tall, distinguished-looking gentleman in a gorgeous cashmere overcoat was changing his ticket for the three o'clock flight the following afternoon. I got in line behind him and was nearly trampled by a herd of my fellow passengers. (I'm under five feet tall, a handicap in a mob scene.) I swiftly calculated the odds of someone helping me versus someone helping an enchanting pug puppy, and I unzipped Clara's bag. Out popped the black head with the bat ears. Sensing my distress, she automatically widened her eyes, cocked her head, and mewed like a dove. Almost instantly, Mr. Cashmere Overcoat took notice and gallantly pushed me to the front of the line. "How old is your pug?" he inquired.

"Eight months," I said.

"I have French bulldogs," he informed me right before he strolled away.

Armed with a return ticket and loaded down with computer and pug, I descended to the baggage claim, the lowest level of hell in this rendition of Dante's *Inferno*. Realizing that they had in their power a way to make the lives of people who had made the mistake of buying a ticket still more difficult, officials announced that we could not leave our bags at the airport unclaimed. It would take "at least" a couple of hours to get the luggage off the plane. Thousands of stranded passengers were having a mass panic attack commandeering taxis, jousting over luggage carts that rented for $1.50 (I vowed if I made it home alive, I would purchase a collapsible cart), bulldozing through pay-phone lines twenty hysterical passengers deep. Curiously, the New Yorkers coped by hollering at anyone who looked remotely official, while the Californians descended as if driven by some primordial force to the rental-car booths.

Clara looked at me reproachfully. She was not content to be dangling from the shoulder bag. It was my duty to restore her to an acceptable level of comfort. She pawed at my purse, and suddenly I remembered that right before we left, Duke had given me a tiny cellular phone as a Valentine's Day present. "What the buffalo was to the Indian, that's what the telephone is to you," he jested. But I loved the idea that I could call for help in a pinch.

The dial tone sounded like the angels singing. I reached the Hotel San Carlos and asked them to save me a room. I didn't have a clue how I was going to get back into Manhattan, but it had to be easier than spending the night in a crowded airport guarding two overstuffed bags I couldn't lift, a computer, and a pug who was unlikely to find grass in the terminal. I visualized us lying on our queen-sized bed eating room-service food and waited for the universe to provide.

Just in case the universe needed help, I released Clara and showed her off to good advantage in my arms. She made herself look extra small and pathetic and gave an anguished whoop. Within three minutes, Mr. Cashmere Overcoat sidled over to her, and within four minutes, Clara was in his arms, licking his face, and my computer was strapped to his cart. Between exclamations about how petite was her body and how perfectly curled was her tail he confided that he had been headed for Los Angeles with two equally tall assistants, whom he had immediately dispatched to the rental-car booth. He gestured to the snaking line to use the phone and grimaced. "I need to call my hotel."

Immediately, I handed him my phone. He stopped stroking Clara long enough to phone a smart hotel on the East Side and tell them that he wanted rooms. Not just any rooms. He wanted his usual suite with the view of Central Park. "You must be a photographer," I noted when he hung up. (I've dated more than my share of photographers and they all maintained a lunatic aesthetic even at the most inopportune moments.)

As a matter of fact, I was talking to Greg German, a

name totally unknown to me at the time but later used by awestruck friends in the question "Not *the* Greg German, celebrity photographer of celebrities?" (He had just finished shooting *the* Arnold.) All I knew at the time was that he was a sucker for a delectable puppy. He offered to drop Clara—and me—off at our hotel. His strapping and resourceful assistants, Kevin and Tom, had managed to rent a minivan. Clara accepted without hesitation. Between their luggage and mine it was a tight fit, but they weren't about to leave Clara. Or the phone. (Me, they would have cheerfully abandoned in a heartbeat, so I took the precaution of mentioning I had an extra battery for the phone in my purse.)

Kevin drove, Tom navigated, Greg and Clara slept in the front seat next to the heater, and I held my breath as the van inched slowly through the unplowed snow on the Van Wyck. They had heard rumors that the bridges were closed, so I called Mother to check. The Triboro was still open, she said, but she felt it was a mistake for me to go back to the hotel. "Have them bring you here," she insisted. I pointed out that her apartment was thirty blocks out of the way. "They're more than welcome to stay here," Mother said.

My rescuers dropped us off in front of the Hotel San Carlos. Clara went into the paws-locked position the instant her feet touched the snowbank, so Greg lifted her up and carried her into the lobby, where again she was welcomed like a foreign dignitary. (She refused to set foot outside the hotel, and so I found her some newspaper.) There was a fax waiting from Duke. "If you are reading this, you win the Urban

Survival Award," it said. Room service was shut down; but Paul magically managed to make Chinese food from Bruce Ho appear, and Clara and I spent the evening snuggling on the bed tuned in to the Storm Watch on television (ironically sponsored by Alaska Cruises). The next day I couldn't get through to American Airlines—I couldn't even get put on hold, just a solid busy signal. The television news reported that Kennedy was scheduled to reopen at four, but I didn't know if our three o'clock flight would go.

I called my husband and asked him to call from Los Angeles. He couldn't get through either. But he was able to get the Kennedy takeoff schedule from an online database and discovered that my flight had a departure time—an hour late, but who cared? Clara and I headed back to the airport and arrived in Los Angeles three and a half hours late. Duke threw his arms around Clara and greeted her joyously. He did not believe she was a rescuer akin to the Saint Bernard who dragged two children from a burning house or the Chesapeake Bay retriever who rescued his five-year-old master from a fast-moving creek.

"Boy, was I smart to get you that phone," he said.